THE Miracle OF INTENT

K P Weaver

Copyright © 2021 K P Weaver

First published in Australia in 2021
by Making Magic Happen Academy

www.makingmagichappenacademy.com
www.karenmcdermott.com.au

All rights reserved. No part of this book may be used or reproduced by any means, graphic, electronic, or mechanical, including photocopying, recording, taping or by any information storage retrieval system without the written permission of the copyright owner except in the case of brief quotations embodied in critical articles and reviews.

Editor: Teena Raffa-Mulligan
Cover and interior design: Ida Jansson

National Library of Australia Cataloguing-in-Publication data:
The Miracle of Intent/Making Magic Happen Academy
Success/Self-help

ISBN (sc): 978-0-6450520-2-2
ISBN (e): 978-0-6450520-3-9

Time is precious so intend with passion.

CONTENTS

Preface	7
Life Intention Bucket List	10
Introduction	13
PART 1: INTENTION SETTING	**17**
Why it is Important to Set Intentions	19
Insight into Intention Setting	23
Five Intention Setting Techniques	28
The Seeds of Intention	35
Intentions and Inspired Thoughts	39
PART 2: THE JOURNEY OF INTENTIONS	**43**
Self-fulfilment in Intention	45
Intention and Gratitude	49
The Journey After Setting an Intention is Not Yours to Control	53
The Block of Worrying About Intentions Not Coming to Fruition	57
Intentions on Getting Ready to Receive	61
PART 3: INTENTIONAL LIVING	**65**
The Importance of Regular Decluttering	67
Sharing Your Intentions with the Right People	72
Intention and Possibilities	77

Acting on Intention	85
Focus and Faith. Are You a believer?	89

PART 4: NEXT LEVEL INTENTIONS — 93

Are You Aware of the Power in Your Intentions?	95
The Colossal Power of a Loving Intention	99
Channelling Intention Through Love	103
Intention and Focus	107
Intention and Cash Flow	112

PART 5: INTENTION AND QUANTUM ENERGY — 117

Universal Thinking and Intentions	119
The Science of Intentions	125
Intention and our Thought Frequency	130
The Miraculous Healing Through Collective Intentions	134
The Self-fulfilling Prophecy When You Live Through the Miracle of Intention	139
The Shift in Energy When You Live Through Intention	143
Conclusion	147

GUEST INTENTION STORIES — 149

Kelly Van Nelson	151
Adrea L Peters	157
Gary Doherty	166
Emma Weaver	174
Peace Mitchell	180

Add to the conversation	*192*

PREFACE

The Miracle of Intent is Book Three of seven in The Alchemy of Life Magic Series. These books are filled with my life principles and share wisdom, knowledge and stories that I hope will inspire, motivate and gift you some valuable tools to enable you to make a difference in your world and reach your highest potential.

These books came about because I was continuously being asked, 'Karen, how do you do life?'

My secrets to life magic are in the pages of these books and I hope they inspire you to write your own stories and discover your own life principles that will be a framework to your perfect balance.

I have invited special guests into these books to share real life experiences of each principle in motion. I set an intention for these books that great stories would be told through them, as my existence is to share stories with the world because stories connect, heal, inspire, educate and so much more. The written word is powerful! When someone reads your words, you have their full attention, they are present without distractions.

Life is for living, it is a huge adventure for us to pursue and see what we can achieve in our lifetime. I know when I leave this earth I will have lived many lifetimes in one. As I write this, I am forty-three and have already experienced more than many people I know. I will leave this lifetime with no regrets and yet I am still only half-way through my life potential.

I never *work* a day in my life, as I *live* my calling and honour my path.

I do not aspire to be famous, but to inspire others to live the best version of themselves. Do you feel that you are living your life to its fullest potential?

If the answer is no, ask yourself, 'Do I want to?' If the answer is yes, then connect with your *Knowing*, set some huge *Intentions* and embrace the journey before you as if you are on the biggest quest of your life. It is our duty to honour our journey, help others along the way, and be the leaders of our own lives so that we can inspire others to be the leaders in theirs. Everyone has the potential to be an inspired leader in their own life. The only leader we need to follow is the leader within ourselves that guides us towards our truest potential. That internal compass has our back, works for our greatest good and helps us live a love-fuelled, passionate life that feels totally aligned with our values, and where no unnecessary fear can reside.

I am a great believer that it is our job in life to serve ourselves first so that we can show up in life, shine, and give our best self to others.

I know the potential of the words in these books, for I live them. I know the potential of what I can achieve and that I have the choice to pursue it or not, and I want you to experience that too.

Let us make magic happen in our lives and the lives of others by embracing these life principles and uniting in leading the way to a future filled with hope, wonder and living at our highest vibration. A world that heals, provides, and unites.

LIFE INTENTION BUCKET LIST

Write below a list of things and experiences you want to achieve in life, adding to it at any point:

INTENTION   DATE ACHIEVED

_____   _____

_____   _____

_____   _____

_____   _____

_____   _____

_____   _____

_____   _____

_____   _____

_____   _____

INTRODUCTION

There are two definitions I would like to share as they will set the scene for what is to come.

A miracle is defined by the Oxford Dictionary as
'an extraordinary and welcome event that is not explained by natural or scientific laws and therefore is attributed to a divine agency.' (I adore this description)

Intention is defined by the Oxford Dictionary as:
'a thing intended, an aim or a plan.'

One of the highest aspects of integrity in my eyes is the origin of a person's intention. I have an internal radar that connects directly with the essence of an intention and determines how I interact with others. I cannot help it, it's in my DNA!

I became aware of this superhuman ability when I saw that other people had different priorities when interacting with others. It is important to me that this is a high priority trait with people in my inner circle and those who I choose to do business with or offer my services. On the few occasions I have welcomed someone into my life without feeling that alignment it has been to my detriment and cost me dearly, because together we were not in flow. Blocks were more frequent and harder to work through.

Setting the intention to surround myself with people who have honest intentions is one of the best life adjustments I ever made. The energy I receive and flow through elevates me and I witnessed an immediate impact on my current circumstance. It really is the most beautiful thing to watch happen and be part of that experience.

I do have to keep a check on myself to make sure my busyness does not overshadow my truest intentions. I always try my best to show up with honest intentions and so far that seems to come across strongly in the channels I show up in, which is both a delight and a relief.

So, I ask you today to take a few minutes to identify if you have the truest intentions for yourself and others and to possibly identify some people in your circle who don't. Set the intention to protect yourself from that energy!

For this book, I set an intention that seemed unattainable, and yet here you are reading it. That shows you that anything is possible with the correct focus and nurtured environment to make it happen.

I hope you enjoy *The Miracle of Intent* and that you will find some golden moments in these pages.

Part 1:
INTENTION SETTING

*Intention is the seed of all reality;
so if you want to change your reality and
discover your true potential, you need
to create a new intention.*

ANDREW WALLACE

WHY IT IS IMPORTANT TO SET INTENTIONS

People with BIG goals are the most alive people I know. I have always enjoyed setting intentions and seeing where life brings me in the pursuit of achieving those goals. I always feel truly alive, my core essence shines bright because I am on an epic adventure. Any adventurer will tell you that yes, the journey is hard work but every bit of it is worth it when you are working towards something you genuinely want to achieve. When I look back on what I have achieved in my life, it's amazing! I am astounded but not surprised by what I have achieved in eight years in business, because I don't see limitations. I set big intentions and pursue them with unwavering faith in my ability to *Know* what opportunities are aligned with my goals and what are not. This gifts me the permission to go forth without fear and on purpose.

I want to share with you a story about my younger sister (and biggest cheerleader), Emma Weaver. My sis has always been passionate about helping others, she has dedicated 26 of her 41 years to it. She is always giving, and showcasing others.

Then it happened, she felt the call to write her story. Step in big sis (me) with her super power of helping people write their stories by eliminating blocks, gifting tips and being efficient with time because let's face it, many of us are time poor!

Well, she did it, she wrote the book and brought it to a place where she could do no more so she handed it over to me and it was sent to my amazing editor, Dannielle. The synergy in that itself was amazing and I must share.

Emma's book was about IVF and her journey was woven through the fictional story. Ultimately, she wrote the book she needed to read at the time. Dannielle had also been through IVF so connected deeply with the book and made it shine. I published the book, positioned my sister well in the market and we launched her. She became an international best-selling author overnight, was being called to do interviews and was on a huge trajectory aligned with her intention of building a mental wealth organisation from scratch. She was getting huge visibility and yet she didn't realise that this would happen by publishing her book. Ultimately, she had set a huge intention to build Mental Wealth International and unknowingly this book was a big part of that.

Do you see what happened here?

The thing that many people don't realise is that intentions are different from goals. Goals you plan, while with intentions you have to be prepared to action aligned opportunities even if you don't fully understand why at the time. The faith in your knowing will ensure your time is not wasted.

When we set an intention, an energetic ball is in motion. Things will shift around you and it's always a good idea to start shedding what no longer serves you so that you have the space in your life for what is to come.

It is important to set intentions because if you don't, you will never know what it is like to make possible what is perceived to be impossible. Now that's fun in motion!

When time and circumstance align, magic happens.

Intention setting is about letting go of the need to control the outcome. It's about being open to receive and letting opportunities flow to you instead of forcing them to happen. It's about action and putting the work in for sure but it's also about trusting the process and allowing the magic to happen in the way that it does, which is not necessarily the same as the picture you originally had in your head. And it's about setting the intention and knowing that everything will unfold exactly as it's meant to.

PEACE MITCHELL,
THE WOMEN'S BUSINESS SCHOOL.

INSIGHT INTO INTENTION SETTING

Why is intention so important in our lives? I would not be where I am today had I not set powerful intentions. We can all set intentions. Intentions…fearless with passion…fearless with purpose…fearless with the awareness that we need to see the bigger picture; to see the opportunities that are aligned with our intentions, our goals, our highest purpose.

Sometimes people set misaligned intentions and that will never make you happy, because you'll never feel truly fulfilled. When I think back to my 20s, I was purpose driven and passionate about everything, but I was totally misaligned.

I didn't know what my calling was, and that was because I hadn't discovered it yet. I was just going through the motions of life and the fallacy of where I could get to.

While I stumbled upon my calling by chance, I don't believe anything is accidental. After a spiritual journey I was open to finding what it was that fulfilled me. And it happened to be writing and sharing stories with the world. It fills me with so much passion.

I'm a publisher but I never studied publishing. My studies are in humanities, and sharing people's stories with the world is what I'm passionate about. Whether it's a children's book, a novel or non-fiction, each story is important because it connects with another person. They're listening to it, learning from it, just having that moment of connection.

One of the final stages of healing for some people is the calling to write their story. That is what happened to me when at the end of October, 2010, I had an epiphany after many years of not knowing why I had had a double miscarriage. Why me? Medical answers didn't give me any reason. I needed a spiritual reason.

One day I was watching a reality TV program called The View and knew I was to watch the next five minutes of the show. There were two special guests on that day, a reality TV couple who had had many miscarriages through IVF. Whoopi Goldberg stopped the show, turned to the woman and said, 'You endured this for a reason; you are not on the right path in life. This was a visitor telling you to get on the right path and your gift will come.'

I was slapped in the face with it. And on that day, I had an amazing urge to share this with the world. I was writing for a website called Building Beautiful Bonds at the time, but a blog did not feel enough.

Then opportunity popped up right in front of my eyes where a novel writing month was starting in two days. Every atom in my body said, *you have got to do this*. It was totally irrational. I had just had my fourth child. She was four weeks old and I was breastfeeding her. I had three other kids that I was very much present with and we hadn't been in Australia for long.

So, you know, I just set that intention to write one thousand six hundred and sixty-seven words a day for thirty days and thought I would see what happened. I knew my current circumstances may not have allowed for it so I wasn't going to pressure myself. But as I always say, where there is a will, there is always a way, and it happened. Thirty days later I had a 50,000-word novel, a first draft, albeit, but a novel. I didn't really know what I was supposed to do with this novel but goodness me, I embraced the learning in that journey.

I am a prolific learner. Whenever I want to learn something, I will find a way and I find my way. When I had a negative experience of publishing I chose to do things my way and I found that my way was being embraced by others. They loved how I was doing things and it led me into becoming a publisher.

Do you see what I'm talking about? The flow. I'm being open and going with it. I'm not setting limitations on what can be achieved. When I set the intention to build Serenity Press into million dollar press, I never imagined that I would be signing Sarah, Duchess of York, or Kate Forsyth, or that I would work with Joanne Fedler.

Do you think for one minute that I thought I would be hiring a castle in Ireland and bringing authors from all over the world to it? That would have probably scared the bejesus out of me at that time because my mindset had not evolved to that space. But at that moment when I set the intention to write a novel in thirty days, I only set the intention to commit to one thousand six hundred and sixty seven words a day.

I never thought I would become an award-winning entrepreneur; that I'd be working with the Duchess of York; that I would be a mum of six. I did not fathom all of this. And I'm glad I didn't know it then because I may have run away. I may not have had the courage to move forward, because at that time my mindset wasn't there. So as I say, whatever intentions you're setting, allow the gift of growth mindset to happen.

Remember, when you're growing, when things are changing and you're evolving as a person, you're going to hit little challenges on your journey. And they're very important challenges because they are going to help you. They're like a little test. They're like little trainings to evolve you to the mindset you need to be for the next stage of development in achieving your highest potential.

So don't say, oh, no, everything's a challenge to do that. Don't have that mindset. That is not a growth mindset. When I won the 2016 Mompreneur Excellence Award, I was asked by the judges, 'What challenges have you endured?' And I thought, challenges are part of my everyday life and I do not see them as negatives because they evolve me into the person I need to be to reach my highest potential to achieve the goals I'm setting. My challenges helped me set the bar higher every time.

Intentions are very, very, very powerful and very important in your life. Set them, but don't limit them.

Setting goals and dreams are all part of life's journey, many of us do this regularly. Setting intentions however is a different matter entirely. This is a much more powerful process, one where you have to feel all the feels and be guided by this. It is imperative that you listen to your inner guide and act on inspired thoughts.

EMMA WEAVER,
MENTAL WEALTH INTERNATIONAL

FIVE INTENTION SETTING TECHNIQUES

There are many ways to manifest your intentions and it's important to know what works for you, what fits how you choose to produce the energy required for opportunities to find their way to you. Yes, they may be a little outside your comfort zone but you will easily identify them as stepping stones to the receipt of your intention, and this is where the magic happens.

I'm going to share five intention setting techniques that might appeal to you. Feel free to explore them yourself. I am all about channelling through my *Knowing* when it comes to my intentions but it can be fun to practise and see what you can make happen with the rest. You might find a practice that works wonders for you.

1. Use Your Imagination.
A concept I was introduced to recently and one that simplifies the act of attraction is called the 'pink bubble effect'. I really like it.

- Close your eyes and think about the one thing you wish you had.
- Keep your eyes closed and role play in your mind a scenario where you have it. Stay there for a moment.
- Now mentally grab a pink bubble and wrap it around your wish.
- Let it go knowing that it is now released and will come back to you at the perfect time.

The magic in this concept is in setting the intention, releasing it and Knowing when to connect and take action towards achieving it. When you set the intention, visualising the outcome and feeling that you have it right now starts the wheels in motion of manifesting the desire. Things will begin to shift around you to make room for what you requested.

   * Shakti Gawain, an internationally renowned teacher of consciousness in her book, *Creative Visualization: Use the Power of Imagination to Create What You Want in Life.*

2. Vision Board

Collect imagery and write down words on a physical or electronic board to create a vision board. To have impact, it's good practice to have it somewhere you can see it every day and also feel what it is like to already have everything on it. Feel it to have it! You need to simply feel what it would be like to have those visions as a reality in your life.

I love vision boards, however I don't put all of my intentional focus onto them, instead I set intentions in motion and live aligned with them every day. For some people vision boards can have an adverse effect as their focus is so fixed on the end goal that they don't connect with the energy essence and so miss the stepping stone opportunities to get there. All they can think of is the end result so they miss the whole point of the journey to receiving.

I do, however, do an annual check-in vision board, especially for my writing. I have MANY book covers pinned to a corkboard for titles waiting to be written. My intention is to end up in a beautiful little house on a hill overlooking a forest with a bay window on the top floor and I write there every day for my readers, both non-fiction and fiction. A home where my grown up children (and their children) can come and go as they please, a home where everyone wants to come for Christmas Day. My heart is doing somersaults writing this.

3. Intention Journal

When you choose to set an intention, writing it down is setting it in motion. It is getting it out of your head and onto paper, initiating an action and therefore a commitment to the pursuit of that intention. As with any journal, you document your thoughts and the journey to receiving your intention. It is often the most magnificent thing to reflect on as you grow and a hugely valuable resource should you ever choose to write your story.

I created my own intention journal several years ago for a few reasons. Firstly, to jot down my intentions; secondly, to have a safe space to record the journey; and thirdly, I wrote 52 intention quotes (one for every week of the year) to inspire others to embrace their intentions.

4. Meditation

In order to connect with intentions that are aligned with our soul purpose, it is important to connect with the essence of who we are at the core. I am blessed with the natural ability of being able to do this due to a year-long inward journey in 2007 that I was guided into through my PTSD experience.

Meditation can be challenging for a busy mind, especially one that likes the busyness; but when you stop and clear the noise around you and in your mind, it is amazing what clarity and connection you can be gifted in this time.

I will never forget the time I went through a guided meditation and experienced excessive heart fluttering when the guide mentioned connecting with the true source of love within. I realised in that moment that the heart palpitations I had been experiencing were not a medical issue, they were in fact a physical reaction to the love of life I was experiencing at the time. Tears of relief trickled down my face. That might sound a little bizarre but the palpitations were so severe I had been put on a heart monitor to investigate the cause of them, but in fact it was my spiritual awakening in motion. This was during my time writing for *Building Beautiful Bonds* and *Universal Mind* magazine.

I now treat writing as my meditative state, a state of mind that I go into where I connect with a higher energy source and allow divine wisdom to flow through me.

Many people see meditation as unachievable because they struggle to silence their mind, but please know it is achievable and the more you do it without high expectations of yourself, the more of a natural process it becomes.

Do it your way and be open to progress so that you can advance your outcomes.

5. Plant an actual intention seed and nurture it to fruition
In this book I use the metaphor of an intention being a seed. Right now I am inviting you to plant an actual seed in the ground and nurture it to fruition. Put love into it and when you tend it, think of the intention you set aligned with that seed.

I planted a frangipani tree in front of my house. It is a tough, resilient tree and when it flowers it is beautiful. It is a representation of the empire I am growing. I nurture it and think positive thoughts when I tend to it. I pour love into it every day. I smile when I see it flower and know that even when it isn't looking so beautiful, there is magic happening on the inside to ensure that it flowers again.

Take a moment to think about a flower or plant that you would like to grow alongside your intention.

No matter how you choose to manifest your intentions it is important to know that unlike goals, an intention will reach its highest level of return when you embark on and embrace the journey. Try not to get distracted by unaligned opportunities that derail you, and the best way to do that is through KNOWING!

To recap on Knowing:

1. Feel it – When you set an intention, opportunities will come your way.
2. Think it – Ask yourself, 'Is this opportunity aligned with my intention?'
3. Action it – If the answer is *yes*, action it straight away; if it is *no* or *not sure*, then dismiss it.

I go in-depth into KNOWING in Book Two of this series, **The Power of Knowing,** where we learn the power in Knowing and how there is no fear in pursuing intentions through this source.

I set the intention to get into the universal laws because I believe that I've been vibrating at a level where I'm attracting a whole lot more than I ever have before.

GARY DOHERTY.
THINK NETWORK AND TEDx CURATOR

THE SEEDS OF INTENTION

'Intention is probably the most underrated and misunderstood phenomenon in terms of fulfilling potential and creating the life you want.'
Andrew Wallace - Intention

This is the first line in an extraordinary little book I discovered when I was researching intention.

One thing that stands out and that I could identify with, as a prolific seed scatterer, is that many of us do not take the time to test the soil in which our intention seeds are being planted. Look at a gardener for example, they make sure the seeds they are sowing are being planted in soil that will give them the best success rate to take root and blossom to their fullest potential.

It is so important when setting intentions that we create a good environment for them to flourish.

We need to be aware of what energy we project onto our intention seeds. Studies have shown that plant seeds given love and spoken to flourished much faster and bloomed more successfully than those that were not. Imagine that, the energy of love and projecting human energy into an actual seed helped it to flourish. It is that type of energy fuel that our intention seedlings need.

How can you attract the opportunities you need that are aligned with your intention at the highest vibration if you are not at your highest vibration? The conditions in which you are planting your seed of intention will not sustain it. When you really nurture your seeds of intention with loving attention, they come to fruition a lot faster.

Sometimes seeds are nurtured for a time before they are planted into the soil and this gives them the best start to take root.

Take a moment to visualise this. The average person has more than 6000 thoughts each day. Imagine how many of them are intentions that we scattered aimlessly over the soil hoping they would take hold. Yet as soon as we walk away the scavenger birds are going to swoop down and gobble them up and maybe one lucky seed will find its way under the surface of the soil. Now visualise having a thought that you treasure, an intention seed that you really want to bring to fruition. You do a little bit of groundwork and help the seed take hold before going to your intention garden and planting it in nourished soil. Then you check in regularly to ensure the soil is kept nourished and the seed has the best chance of reaching the surface when you can watch it grow before your eyes, taking action when needed but witnessing the fruits of your labour blossom.

Those intentions are what life is all about, they make your heart sing, they are intentions that don't happen every day, they are big milestones in life and they are worth celebrating.

Be mindful that when you have an intention that you really want to happen, do the work at the start. Tap into your intuition of what that intention seed needs, do some research to give it the best chance and then when time and circumstance align, the magic will happen. You will be the one who benefits because you own the seed, you nurtured it to fruition and so you will reap the rewards.

When we set an intention, things will start to shift around us for it to find its way to us and quite often we have to start a process of clearing because our lives are too full.

K P Weaver

INTENTIONS AND INSPIRED THOUGHTS

Intentions and inspired thoughts. What a powerful combination, I truly adore watching the process.

It can be misconceived that when we set an intention, we wait for an opportunity to present itself to us aligned with that intention, and that we just have to be aware that

1. The opportunity is aligned with our intention, and
2. That we have the courage to act straight away if it is.

That is not the only way to facilitate an intention.

Inspired thoughts are gifts from the universe that plant in our mind for a moment for us to action immediately because as quickly as they come into our mind, they can leave again. We are left with a residue of, 'What was that amazing thought I had, I wish I had written it down.' Can you relate?

I have actioned and reaped the rewards of MANY inspired thoughts. I signed the Duchess of York to Serenity Press because of an inspired thought after setting an intention to make my publishing press more visible. The result is the most beautiful connection with the Duchess, a twenty-two-book deal, and our press was featured in hundreds of publications across the world.

Another time I set an intention to have Elizabeth Gilbert feature in one of my books, so I acted on an inspired thought, showed up at each step of the journey to it happening and made it easy for a yes decision.

One of the best pieces of advice I can give anyone about actioning thoughts is that when you action a seedling of an idea, and you get a response, make it easy for the main people involved to say yes. Most people or businesses who have 'made it' need things to flow easily. Any sign of reluctance or a potential block might hinder a positive outcome.

And of course people who set intentions that are aligned with their values, which includes connecting with people of similar values, ensures that any outcome will feel worthwhile and without compromise.

Inspired thoughts come ready for you to act on them immediately! Please don't fall into the slippery slope of overthinking an inspired thought. You simply action it with your first impulse.

*We go inwards for the answer and outside for
the support to make it happen.*

Be confident in your inspired thoughts. Other people might not understand them and may even judge them as being unconventional, but leave that with them, don't take it on board, let the results speak for themselves. You are guaranteed results when you have the courage to act on inspired thoughts.

To conclude this chapter, inspired thoughts are gifts. They are gifts that bring you inward to think and subsequently action an interaction that will advance you towards your intentions.

Part 2:

THE JOURNEY OF INTENTIONS

This principle of intention is literally what saved and changed the trajectory of my living.

OPRAH WINFREY

SELF-FULFILMENT IN INTENTION

I believe, no, in fact I know that if I had not first journeyed within and connected to my true self, really stopped to take time to get to know the real me and what makes me tick, then I would not have the aligned ability to make powerful intentions.

I have written before on how I ventured within. It wasn't a choice, it was as the result of circumstance but what I first deemed to be trauma ended up being a sabbatical into the inner workings of myself. I have in fact discovered a deeper meaning to my life all because I decided to seek the light in the darkness.

I set the intention to find the positive in a negative situation and this ensured that my PTSD was a journey and not a waste of my life experience but an advancement. I felt blessed because many people can get stuck in the trenches of PTSD and it can often define a lifetime. For me it was one year and it taught me how to turn challenges into opportunities to grow and I will be forever grateful.

The intention I set back then showed me how powerful intentions are. I could never have known the way out of the darkness had I not been in tune with who I was and had a belief that I was strong enough. The mind is very powerful, it is what stands between us succeeding and failing. When I intended inwards I discovered what truly fulfilled me, and that was not influenced by any outside influences. That is a truly deep and fulfilling experience.

Now, when I set an intention I seek inside myself for the answer and then when I have done all that I can, I lean outwards to others for support to move forward. When we are self-fulfilled through intention it means that we know exactly what opportunities to say yes to, especially because venturing inside we also reconnect with our natural born ability to Know.

It's important to be self-fulfilled when manifesting through intention or really, what is the point? Intentions take time, energy and quite often investment to make them happen. They are not for the faint hearted. However, they are fun and very fulfilling when you feel the glow from within when you make a dream come true.

One of the things that gets me is when I see someone set a HUGE intention only for them to not understand the power of going inward to navigate it. No one is more in tune or invested in your ambitions than you. Others will join you on the journey for part of the way or from start to finish but you are the one who is most invested in the outcome. Never give someone else the power over the outcome of your intentions as they will never manifest the perfectly aligned opportunities that you will and to be honest, there is not as much fulfilment in someone else making something happen for you. They can serve you well if you delegate to them but as for the driving seat, that's yours.

One of the highest aspects of integrity in my eyes is the origin of a person's intention.

K P Weaver

INTENTION AND GRATITUDE

Intentional gratitude is a divine energy to live through. When you are grateful with intention people often respond with the same gratitude in return. Refreshingly, it is a more dominant trait of human nature. I have witnessed gratitude in motion through hosting a 365-day gratitude challenge in my Life Magic group on Facebook and I never cease to be amazed by how some people can remain filled with gratitude even when faced with adversity.

    I will speak more in-depth about gratitude in *The Gift in Gratitude* but felt it important to share the connection with intention.

When we are grateful for the little things as much as the big things, it helps us fast track the energy and the vibration and brings us into that receiving space. Although many people don't give with the intention to receive, it is a welcome return and of course linked to the Law of Reciprocation.

Gratitude through intention brings us into a higher vibration of gratitude and of love, because there's lots of love in gratitude.

Some people show gratitude through prayer which of course is taking time to be intentional about the positives and also find solace in the pain. Personally, I like to end my day by reflecting on what's happened and noting what I'm grateful for during that day. In the same way I try to be intentional about how I begin my day. I start early, doing something I love (writing), because it sets my day in a powerful positive motion.

I recommend that you ask yourself, *'What am I grateful for today?'* and if the answer is, *'Nothing,'* you need to adjust your mindset. No matter how small, there is something to be grateful for every day! And the more you practise intentional gratitude, the more natural it becomes and the more you'll identify what a positive it is in your life. I am intentionally grateful every single day for both big and small things and each day that list grows.

I always ask that we acknowledge both because you're emitting the same energy into the universe either way, and what we perceive to be the little graces in life are often the biggest treasures. So with that intention and the gratitude and the perspective you have, you are keeping it real and that will help you stay connected to your authentic self.

Life can change in an instant, but you will always have something to be grateful for.

So in those tough moments - because let's be honest, we all have them — be mindful to be intentionally grateful and your vibration won't sink as low as it could and you will bounce back in record time.

An intention precedes every thought and every action, and the outcome of your experiences is determined by the intention.

OPRAH WINFREY

THE JOURNEY AFTER SETTING AN INTENTION IS NOT YOURS TO CONTROL

In 2019 I set an intention to get my teeth fixed. My teeth never survived having six children and when pregnant with my fifth child five teeth shattered in my mouth. It had come to the point where I had no teeth at the two sides of my mouth, only stumps, and my front teeth were constantly moving. My mouth was so unhealthy and my breath smelled terrible. I would wake in the middle of the night with lots of blood in my mouth. I had toothaches so bad the pain went right up the side of my face and into my head.

As I set the intention to get my teeth sorted once and for all I was open to the opportunity to make that happen. I was told I was at a high risk of stroke because of how bad my teeth were and it was advised that I get them out and replaced. Having a young family, this was a wake-up call! There was also family history of strokes so I wasn't prepared to take any chances. My children needed me to be my best self for them.

I explored some avenues and had some work done but ultimately it was all leading back to the same scenario, one that I didn't enjoy the thought of but knew I would have to accept and endure. I was scheduled to have my teeth removed and replaced one month before I was due to co-host a huge corporate event in an Irish castle.

I will never forget the day of the procedure. I dropped my kids off at school and drove to the dentist. I had successfully put it out of my head until then. The reality hit while I was sitting in the waiting room but I was steadfast. I was scheduled to have the procedure done in stages but I'm so glad the dentist appreciated my personal situation and offered to do it all at once. My dentist was really amazing, he made me feel at ease and I am sure it was traumatic for him too, I could see it in his eyes when it was all over hours later. I did not feel any pain, I was awake the whole time. The biggest challenge was to keep my mind occupied, but I did and truly got to see my strength.

I was surprised that afterwards the pain was not as bad as I had expected. My mouth was sore and I couldn't take the high dose painkillers prescribed as I needed to be alert at all times for my children and also do school runs. But there was an aspect I wasn't prepared for and that was the grief I felt. I never expected it! It caught me off guard and sank me into sadness, real death sadness.

I needed to honour the process of physical healing and now also emotional healing. My kids were so beautiful, they took care of me and knew that Mummy wasn't feeling well. The thing about having lots of girls is that they love playing nurse. They kept my spirits up and with a trip home to Ireland to look forward to I had a deadline for when I wanted to feel better. It was the distraction I needed.

It was so worth it, as I feel healthier and I can now smile with pride. When I look back on the pictures from that trip I don't see sadness, I see a happy heart and a beautiful smile and I am grateful that I saw it through.

You see, one thing to be mindful of when setting intentions is that you will not know what you are signing up for beforehand. Yes, you are in the driving seat and call the shots but if you are truly dedicated to achieving the intention you set, the opportunities that present themselves to you may not be ideal yet are necessary.

Intentions are a commitment to an end result. Goals are planned, intentions are embraced.

The thing that many people don't realise is that intentions are different from goals. Goals you plan, while with intentions you have to be prepared to action aligned opportunities even if you don't fully understand why at the time. The faith in your knowing will ensure your time is not wasted.

K P Weaver

THE BLOCK OF WORRYING ABOUT INTENTIONS NOT COMING TO FRUITION

Thinking too much about what people will think if you don't achieve your intentions can be a huge block in the process of achieving what you intend. And to be honest people are way more interested in themselves than worrying about you and what you said you were going to do. Also, there is no set timeframe on how long an intention needs to come to fruition.

Lots of people hold back on setting intentions and therefore do not reach their highest potential because of the fear of failure, the fear of not achieving. And what I say to that is, how are you supposed to reach your highest potential if you don't keep moving forward, learning, growing through every challenge? You're learning something so you never actually fail.

One of my good friends and authors, Ron Malhotra, in his book *Impossible to Fail* says even failure is winning because you learn so much from failing. If you've done something and failed, you're not starting from scratch again. You're starting from the point where you left off. Your starting point is from more advanced knowledge, you're starting ahead of the game because your mindset and perspective are stronger than before.

I want you to consider that when you're holding back on your intentions. One of the keys to achieving your highest potential is setting intentions, and if you don't set intentions, especially when they are inspired, then you're missing out on life. I don't want you to miss out on life, and this book is all about giving; gifting you the tools so that you don't miss out on living your best life.

Remember that when you are connected to a *Knowing* there is no fear, so you can never fail embracing this life principle. Yes, there will be some seeds that do not come to fruition. Yes, you may talk about them in your arena and people may notice, but you know what? Really and truly, nobody is bothered. Everyone is too busy thinking of themselves. And if they do say something, it's not the end of the world. Stay positive and don't worry about what they say because it will soon be yesterday's news.

One key component is, never admit defeat because there is no defeat, there is just divine timing. There is power in knowing that, for when the time is right, things fall into place more easily. Believe in divine timing and success is the next natural step forward because you have evolved into the person you need to be to receive that intention.

Your job is to prepare yourself for that and not worry about what other people think. Do not hold back because I promise, you will get there when the time is right; and the quicker you evolve and move forward, the quicker that time will come for you. And I want that time to come for you. When you see people who have built the momentum, they have many years behind them or they have really good mentors behind them who are able to help save them time.

People who are investing in themselves, good mentors and people who have achieved great things are amazing. But you know what? They're not going to guide someone to achieve the same as them. They're going to guide their mentees, their clients to see the potential in themselves and find their own way. Not the mentor's way, because you can learn from leaders and mentors, but you can never copy what they do because they have done it their way.

You have to find your way. A good mentor will always help you find your way because that's what's sustainable. That's what changes the mindset and that is what changes your future if you're in it for a long-term gain.

You do not need to let fear hold you back from certain intentions, because if you don't try, you're never going to know what you can achieve.

Know what that feeling is. That miraculous feeling is when an intention happens that is absolutely aligned.

Our intention creates our reality.

WAYNE DYER

INTENTIONS ON GETTING READY TO RECEIVE

Quite often when we set an intention we are not ready to receive it. In that I mean that often we set big intentions and have to go on a journey to become the person we need to be to align ourselves with the receipt of that intention.

I have set huge intentions, big fat shiny intentions that are huge dreams. What I have come to discover many times is that when the right time and circumstance align for us to receive that intention, we have evolved to such a place in our existence that the receipt of that intention feels like the next natural step in life.

I cannot emphasise enough that when we set an intention we are also committing to the journey that comes along with the self-development that will happen. If you are resistant you will feel a huge struggle so it is very important to understand that setting an intention is not to be taken lightly. When you set an intention, it sends a powerful vibration out from you, a signal that you have an important request, and that sets things in motion so you will begin to feel things shifting around you. It's always a good time to do a life declutter at this point so that you free up some time, space and energy to embrace the opportunities that come your way.

So your job in the intention setting process is to:

1. Make sure the intention you set is something you really want to put your energy into and achieve in your life.
2. Know that things will change so be mindful that what you are attracting does not jeopardise the things you treasure.
3. Never compromise your values.
4. Know when to say yes and when to say no.
5. Learn to enjoy the journey.

So, if receiving an intention is often a struggle then why bother?

The answer to that is simple. Whenever you receive something that's absolutely aligned, it feels natural. It feels like, yes, I should be getting this right now. And you can never know the euphoria of this experience until you start receiving big things and they feel so natural. It won't feel overwhelming, it will feel aligned within you and in your whole life.

Whenever we set a big intention/dream, what the laws of

attraction do not tell us is that we need to prepare ourselves to act when the aligned opportunity presents itself. It is not a case of setting an intention and getting on with life until it drops in your lap. We need to put the work in behind the scenes so that we can become the people we need to be to receive that gift, that wish, that goal, that intention.

If we don't, how are we supposed to give it our best? How are we supposed to get the most out of receiving it if we are not perfectly aligned with it? This is such an important message. We are ever evolving as humans. When we set big goals, we evolve at a faster rate when we fuel them with loving intention, we supercharge them. I know from my own experience that when I am evolving at a faster rate, there are moments of feeling unsettled.

You know, those times when you feel unsettled within yourself but you can't put your finger on it. I have come to identify that we should not fear this feeling as it comes every time we are evolving, it is an internal transition. My energy is transitioning and I no longer fear it, I trust that it will pass. There has been a simple adjustment of shifting my perception of the feeling and mindfully allowing it to pass instead of taking unnecessary action that might jeopardise the fruits of my labour that are about to occur. I now know with all my heart that I'm evolving into something which is exciting and nothing to fear. And then as the discomfort passes I get that magic feeling, which is wonderful because I can feel it happening. The energy fills me with a cocktail of love, excitement, and gratitude. But you can only know that feeling when you stay the course and it's not something you can describe. It's something that you just know. And you really must be open to that kind of thinking and that kind of awareness of yourself to really understand. It's not *woo woo*, it's also science!

And, you know, I am brave enough to say it, but because I've lived it, I've done it many times and it is a pattern I have identified, I want everyone to benefit from this awareness. So yes, you will feel unsettled but that's as bad as it gets. Do not fear that feeling because if you do you are probably going to take an action that will impede your results. If you have ever read *The Five Stages of the Soul* by David Carroll and Harry R. Moody, you will understand that before any worthwhile breakthrough there's always the struggle. The key to reaching the breakthrough is to grow through the struggle.

Part 3:

INTENTIONAL LIVING

> When our actions are based on good
> intentions our soul has no regrets.
> ANTHONY DOUGLAS WILLIAMS

THE IMPORTANCE OF REGULAR DECLUTTERING

When we set an intention, things will start to shift around us for it to find its way to us and quite often we have to start a process of clearing because our lives are too full. You'll find things that no longer serve you start to fall away. If we don't allow those things to filter away, then we become overwhelmed because there's too much going on in our lives. Don't hoard life!

I know this because I have done this. I have kept taking on, taking on, taking on, without stopping to intentionally declutter my life from the debris of things that do not serve me anymore. I have discovered that it is a really good habit for me to do this regularly. It used to be every year, then reduced to six months, and is probably going to be every three months soon because things are moving at a faster pace.

When you build momentum, when you set big intentions in motion, when you're doing lots of things, it's important to keep decluttering as you go along. You don't want to hold onto stuff that doesn't serve you anymore because it wears you down and depletes your energy, and in order to keep achieving, you want to live at a high vibration and won't want anything to bring your frequency down. That is why it is super important to stop and declutter. It is good practice if with every intention you set, you let something go. That way you have the opportunity to choose instead of being forced to let go of something you want to hold onto.

It's so important because if you don't, you may get overwhelmed, you will be too far in and might even end up getting sick as a result of doing too much. You risk burnout.

Consider also that your rubbish may be somebody else's treasure. If there is something in your life that no longer serves you, pass it on or sell it to somebody else who will value it. I promise you, there will be somebody who will see value in it.

It's imperative that you step back and let go or create a divide there because you don't need that energy pulling you back, it doesn't serve you when you are setting intentions. To supercharge forward you need to get to the realm of a high vibrational energy field. So in that light, please honour that and undo the clutter as you go along.

When you start these amazing intentions, how is the magic of them supposed to shine into your life if everything is too full? Look at your life as a sphere around you and you are in there living your life. If your life is jam-packed, how can the magic shine in?

My four top tips for decluttering your life are:

1. Write a comprehensive list of EVERYTHING that takes up your time right now. (Work towards letting go of what no longer serves you on that list).
2. Consider where you are focusing your energy. Is it positive? Does it recharge you? Can you let go of some of that energy commitment now? Maybe give it less energy?
3. Remember to always keep your core values close to your heart and make all decisions through that funnel.
4. Remember some things and people are only in your life for a season, it does not serve you or them/it if you hold on for longer.

When you intentionally create the space and declutter to make room it will lighten you. You will feel instantly freer and may even decide not to fill up the space quite so much next time. If you're in business, delegating can be your best friend. For me and my business, growth happened when I learned how to delegate, which meant I could stay in my genius zone, doing what I love. Dream scenario right there! By mindfully setting an intention to create the space, things began to flow more naturally. I do the same when I am writing my books. I declutter to salvage the much-needed time to create and I also prioritise my writing. It is important to me to find time to write these books and share them with you, which means that I also must give myself permission to prioritise it as much as I would a business appointment. Even, for the period of time

I am writing, I gift myself permission to not do so many extra family activities. My children are perfectly happy playing in our backyard, or using their imagination playing with their dolls' house, or even (my favourite) let them get bored because that is when creativity flourishes. I do adore those words, 'Mum, I'm bored.' I always offer to alleviate that boredom by finding them a chore to do. Funny how that initiates a creative mind.

You will get amazing results from decluttering but be mindful of your energy because some things we let go of need us to take a moment to honour them and maybe even grieve the loss. They will have served us and it is now time to move on so it is important to process and release any emotions connected to that. Don't just suppress the feelings, block them off and heartlessly move forward. Honour the feelings that come to the surface and allow the grief to pass through you so that you free yourself and don't have any residue lingering after you move on.

I know lots of people who volunteer their time and that is wonderful. I volunteer for lots of things, but everything I volunteer for serves me where I am at that period in my life and therefore it adds to my pot. When something begins to take away from my pot, then it is time to move on and let someone else have the opportunity to evolve through the opportunity. It doesn't serve you or them to hang on after it is time to go. Is there something you are doing right now that you can move on from?

*When we set intentions aligned with our
core values we never have to compromise.*

K P Weaver

SHARING YOUR INTENTIONS WITH THE RIGHT PEOPLE

However you choose to set your intentions, sharing them with the right people will ensure that you stay committed and maybe even get some support to make your dreams become reality.

Some of the people to share with are:
- Your cheerleaders
- The media
- Family who support your dreams
- Decision makers in the arena of your intentions
- Yourself on a regular basis.

People who it is best not to share with:
- People who do not get it.
- Competitors
- Those jealous of others' success.

So why share your intentions at all?

There are pros and cons to sharing your intentions, especially in the early stages but I believe the pros outweigh the cons, so when an intention starts to take hold it is good to put it out there amongst the right people.

There have been times that I wished I had not shared but that was because I shared too early. I now know the right time to share is when the thought evolves in my mind. If I have a seedling of an idea, I give it time to germinate in my mind and if it is still there probing at me a few days later, well there is something in it.

Let those you love and spend the most time with understand that your focus may be diverted because you have set an intention. When you have their support, it's great, when you don't it's not as easy but still not necessarily a block. I highly recommend only letting the positive, supportive energy in.

In my experience if you are upfront and say that whatever it is, is important to you then they will come round. Some people don't like the thought of something changing and so there might be some resistance but remember it is your intention, not theirs. My partner was not always supportive of my intentions, they were huge, and I understand how overwhelming that can be to load onto others who don't share the passion. But stick it out if it means a lot to you.

Sharing with the people who *get it* is a very important

aspect, especially when you feel the urge to share with someone, and our intuition guides us to who to tell. Intentions are more powerful when you share them with people who can help make them real.

Some people may say you're procrastinating when you talk about an intention and it doesn't come to fruition straight away, but I don't believe that because it is not up to us to determine when the time and circumstance aligns for our dreams to become reality. We just need to keep showing up and not abandon the idea at the eleventh hour. I see too many dreams abandoned in what could be a moment before a breakthrough. The missing ingredient is faith. You are setting the scene and setting an intention that gathers the vibration and starts to become a reality.

The key ingredient here is that you must tell the right people.

If you are the type of personality (like me) who is stubborn and when people say that something isn't possible, it fuels the fire to go for it more, then you won't be daunted by the non-believers, the un-supporters, the people who use their energy to pull you down instead of using it to lift themselves up, so share away. They are equally important to your journey because we know that anything is possible when we put our minds to it!

So it's very important when you have the courage to share an intention in the world that you share with the right people so they add to your vibrational energy that goes into that intention so that it can reach far and wide. That vibrational energy is also actionable energy, because if they understand what it is that you're wanting to achieve, they may have the absolute desire to help you achieve it.

Good people do that. For example, I never anticipated that

a conversation I had with someone would lead to my dream of being asked to speak on a TEDx stage. And when I chatted with him, I never expected him to ask me to be on his stage. But it happened through having the courage to share my intentions with the right people and by genuinely showing up, it led to a natural progression that flowed into a dream.

 Share your intentions with *your* people, not just with anybody, and they will pick up momentum, they will expand vibrationally and energetically become a tangible product of your thoughts and actions. By owning the intention you are putting it out there. But put it out there with the right people so they can help you!

By banishing doubt and trusting your intuitive feelings, you clear a space for the power of intention to flow through.

Wayne Dyer

INTENTION AND POSSIBILITIES

Possibility is a product of setting strong intentions. We must be open to infinite possibilities when we intend to achieve great things. It is important to be mindful that they will come from the most unforeseen places. In my eyes an intention is so much bigger than a goal because a goal is something that you plan meticulously to reach an end result. There are usually planned steps on how to achieve that goal and all focus is on putting each one of those steps in motion. When you set an intention, you fuel it with energy to go out into the world with the hope of the end result. And I see hope in a powerful sense, as in being open to the result and trusting that it is going to be bigger than you can ever imagine so you are not limiting the possibilities of what can be achieved.

The reason I talk about this is because if I had limited my intention for setting up a million dollar press I could never have fathomed the journey, the interactions and the connections I have made. I don't want you to set limits, because with an intention, our job is to show up. Our job is to have the courage to take action when aligned opportunities come our way. And it's not up to us to determine how we achieve that.

Intention is a meaningful thought that we set in motion by fuelling it with positive energy and being on call to action aligned opportunities that will reveal themselves to us. How it's going to manifest is not our job. Absolutely know what is aligned with that intention and have the courage to say yes to it; and equally have the courage to say no to things that are distracting along the way. When you are aligned with your intentions, your values and your absolute core essence of who you are, there's no greater feeling in the world! I am going to say that again because I need it to sink in.

> *When you are aligned with your intentions, your values and your absolute core essence of who you are, there's no greater feeling in the world!*

You can easily identify people who are aligned because they shine, they're confident and they fit the skin they're in. They shine this brightly because they are living in a very high vibration, they have done the inner work and are now reaping the rewards and you cannot fake that. I am not talking about a fake confidence often found with Instagram-built influencers.

Are they really that happy? True inner core happiness shines. It's an energy. It's a glow. It's a magical essence. You can see and feel it around someone, whether they are in front of you or behind a screen.

And yes, lots of influencers may have wonderfully aligned and branded content on social media. But are they happy, truly happy at their core essence? True happiness, true essence, magic and true fulfilment comes from being aligned with your life's purpose and being open to all of the possibilities that come with that.

I could not have achieved what I have had I not been open to possibilities. Remaining consistently open minded becomes second nature and you come to understand that there are no limitations.

Let me tell you a story about when I set an intention to do a TEDx talk.

I aligned with my life magic principles. I know the power of when I set an intention and just put it out there. I keep it always at the back of my mind that I'm aware of opportunities aligned with that intention.

It is our job when setting intentions to prepare ourselves so that whenever that intention comes your way, you're ready to grasp it with both hands. When it's a supersonic big fat intention, then you will have a lot of development to do, so I had lots of opportunities to speak and connect to crowds and see how people react to my words.

I put my whole loving intention into it, as I do with everything I choose to do. I did the groundwork, I got myself TEDx stage ready so that when the opportunity arose I would be ready to grab it with both hands.

So here I was, big intention set, absolutely aligned with

that happening, ready and trusting that when time and circumstance aligned, the magic would happen.

And then out of nowhere an opportunity to apply for a talk came, but I didn't get it and actually didn't feel aligned with it either. Then another opportunity came along that was local to me. I applied but didn't get that either. Somehow neither felt right anyway. Although I honour processes, I always knew within me that this was not the way for me, and I don't know why. I suppose it's because of how I do life, how I make the big things in my life happen. They're never done the conventional way…ever!

So I had a little conversation with myself: *'Karen, you know how to do this, keep the intention close and get on with life as it is and the opportunity will present itself to you by being mindfully aware of all interactions that come your way. Just be you and it will happen. Relax, it's coming!'*

My subconscious mind was right, I always happen to position myself in the right place at the right time…or ask the right person…or have courage to ask…or a connection I have will approach me with an unexpected opportunity. So I got on with life. It was a super busy time for me in publishing so I jumped in and cleared some beautiful projects off my to-do list. And I began to feel lighter and happened to declutter my surroundings, which is always freeing and often clears a block somewhere because when our heart's desires start to come to fruition there needs to be space to enjoy it to its best potential.

Then my TEDx intention was set in motion. My sister introduced me to someone to have a chat with and my aim was to connect and see how I could help him. I was tired that night (it was a UK call) but I showed up and had the best conversation with a truly like-minded person. We talked way longer than expected but it was good and I always love sharing my knowledge with others. I was grateful to meet someone with fire in their belly. The next day when I woke up, there was a message on my phone: *'I couldn't stop thinking about our conversation and I would like to ask you if you would be on my TEDx stage.'* Well, does that even happen! I was blown away. By showing up and being myself I secured my dream of a TEDx talk. Now that's how I do life!

I obviously said, *'YES! By hook or by crook, I'm going to be there.'* I was going to be in Ireland anyway in January so could absolutely do the talk. Little did I know COVID-19 would affect my plans. Living in Perth, Western Australia, is wonderful because we don't have community spread here, but we also don't have the freedom to leave and return to the state. And as I said, I don't compromise on intentions that are aligned and balanced with my values and my family life, because it's important to me.

I realised I would have to approach the curator and let him know that I couldn't be on his stage. Going to Ireland meant I would have to quarantine on the way back and miss my daughter's first day of high school. That would go against one of my core values of not missing key milestones in my kids' life.

I was sad that I wouldn't be able to be on that stage and my TEDx talk might not happen, but in my heart I felt like something was not falling apart, it was actually coming together!

I could have chosen to feel sorry for myself but I chose to sit in the energy of my dream scenario instead.

'I am putting this out there. I would love to be able to do the talk from a stage in Perth because I really wanted the experience

of going onto a stage. I would love to do it this year because I am ready now and it was a 2020 goal; and I would love to do a TEDx women's event because I just won the Ausmumpreneur Women Will Change the World Award and that all feels truly aligned.'

I loved the feeling that scenario gifted me.

Well, what happened next BLEW my mind! And remember here, I never get easily shocked because I know that ANYTHING is possible. The NEXT DAY I got a message, and it went something like this…

'Hi Karen, I have been asked to host a TEDx women's event in eight weeks' time. It would mean that you will have to film from a stage in Perth but I would love for you to be one of the speakers.'

Need I write anything more? And to put the cherry on the top, my beautiful sister Emma was also going to be a speaker! I felt like I had won the life Lotto.

On November 20th 2020 my TEDx talk, Own Your Story, Change Your Life went live and I hope that it reaches the hearts of those who need to watch it.

So what can we learn by this example of intention in motion?

Firstly, that we don't give up on our intentions, we evolve with them. When we set intentions we may feel challenged at times but that happens to help us to grow into the person we need to be to receive. When time and circumstance align is the perfect time to receive, and the faster we choose to embrace the discomfort of personal growth and evolve throughout the process, the quicker we achieve our heart's desire!

It's not up to me to determine what is possible. It's up to

me to determine what I want and how I want it and to make sure that I'm all in and maintain a high vibration to receive. I always keep open to the possibility of everything working out. I choose to never wallow in self-pity or sadness because of fear, I choose to embrace my knowing that the universe provides and it is providing exactly how it needs to provide.

And I don't have to sacrifice any of my values to make it happen because that goes against my life principles. So I tell you this story, hoping that it inspires you because it's an important story. Not just for me, but so that you understand that there are no limitations. The possibilities are miraculous! And to bring us back to the definition of a miracle…*'an extraordinary and welcome event that is not explained by natural or scientific laws and therefore is attributed to a divine agency.' Oxford Dictionary.*

So set your intentions and allow them to find their way to you by being courageous, stepping up and taking action and never letting go of the belief that there is the possibility of a miracle.

*When you have clarity of
intention the universe conspires with
you to make it happen.*

FIABIANNE FRIEDRICKSON

ACTING ON INTENTION

People who make it are not the overnight sensations we deem them to be, it takes a lot of navigating to position yourself for success. One true overnight success story I like to share is that of Spanx founder Sara Blakely. I absolutely get this woman. Her passion, focus, drive and most importantly, unwavering Knowing shines through. I recently watched an interview she did with Tony Robbins and to listen to her share every aspect of her journey to shine the light for others made my heart swell with delight.

The focus was not on her big breakthrough when Oprah brought her on the show. The focus was on how she navigated a breakthrough with getting her product into a chain of seven stores in the US. Sara didn't know how it was usually done eg via trade shows etc. Her instinct said to call and not leave a message, but to get someone on the other end in the buying department to answer and secure a 10-minute slot with them. She flew there and five minutes in she knew she was losing her buyer so she took action straight away and said, 'Can you come to the bathroom with me.' She used herself as a model to show her Spanx under white trousers and then also without them. The visual got her the deal, gave the buyer the impact they needed to say yes.

But let's talk about the idea and how it came to be in the first place. Sara was a salesperson for many years before the Spanx idea came to her. She describes a tear-filled desperate moment in which she felt like she was in the wrong movie, looked up to the universe and asked for an idea for her own product to sell. One day after cutting the legs out of some pantihose Sara realised that was her idea and so she ran with it.

After getting the seven stores on board she actually paid her friends to go in and buy the products. She also drove to every store during a 21-day road trip, spent the day there and got the staff excited about her product. Sara sold directly to customers and her bubbly nature was embraced on many levels. She got actionable! Even after being on Oprah's show, Sara has remained a close friend with her customers and is very proactive in her business.

We can learn so much from this story about the process of intention and I strongly recommend that you watch the interview. You will witness intention in action. Sara encompassed each one of the life principles I speak on in this series.

1. **Mindfulness:** She was mindful of the opportunities coming to her and mindful to take action.
2. **Knowing:** Listen to her story; you will know that she followed her Knowing!
3. **Intention:** She absolutely set a powerful intention and stuck to it.
4. **Gratitude:** She was so grateful for every opportunity and took nothing for granted. Gratitude is currency when it comes to opportunity.
5. **Love:** By goodness did she not (and still does) pursue this with loving intention!
6. **Forgiveness:** She held no grudges, she learned and moved on. This gifted her the freedom to move forward with nothing holding her back!
7. **Belief:** She absolutely believed in her product and herself because it wasn't about her, it was about helping women feel good, it became her mission.

I would like you to take a moment to think about how you do life. Is there something you can learn from Sara's story, or someone else who you look up to, that you can apply to your own life? Learn from people like Sara who takes ownership of her own life and goes for it. We can all get inspired by others but what we do with that inspiration, how we interpret that in our own lives to fuel our intentions is what will make us stand out from the crowd. Be inspired, be innovative, be open-minded.

*Our intention is everything,
nothing happens on this planet without it.*

Jim Carrey

FOCUS AND FAITH. ARE YOU A BELIEVER?

Do you believe in the power of intention? It can be hard to believe in something if you can't see it with your eyes or feel it with your hands. Yet the most amazing things that have happened in my life have come from having faith that all will turn out exactly as it is meant to, and that I will show up and go on the journey when needed to move things along.

I one hundred percent believe in the magic of intention. There is science in it but I love to think of the magic in it too.

One thing we do not want to do is feed into the cycle of overthinking as that often leads to analysis paralysis and that serves no one.

Had I overthought when I set the intention to write my first novel in 2010 it would not have happened and had that not happened, I would not have found my true calling and path into publishing. It does not bear thinking about!

But the seed was planted when a conversation I had with a friend gifted me the belief that writing a novel was possible. I had limiting beliefs around that, which I had to shatter. When I started to believe in the possibility, I also became more open minded and aware of the signs coming my way that led to writing my first book. Once that limiting belief was dispelled there was nothing holding me back. No excuses could be made, possibility grew into potential and subsequently a series of serendipitous events led to me sitting down at my computer on November 1st 2010 to write 1667 words a day for 30 days and produce a first draft of my first novel.

None of this would have been possible if I did not have faith in the outcome and believe that it was possible. And if I failed it was not the end of the world because at least I had tried.

So many people cannot see past their own limitations, quite often stemming from childhood. That is OK if those beliefs serve us as adults but when they don't, we need to do the work to unlearn them and release the control they have on our mind. When that happens in your life it changes you from the person you were before, to the person you now are. It is a truly instant and magical feeling. One to treasure!

There's nothing like that feeling of knowing when something is absolutely aligned and you get an inspired thought. You may have to have courage to action it but you have unwavering knowledge that it is aligned with the intention that you set. It's so important when the inspired thoughts or opportunities come to you that you have created the right vibrational frequency. It means that you can reach the highest heights with your intentions.

When time and circumstance align, that is when the magic happens. So set your intention, be patient, be aware, be focused and watch as the results come rolling in. Focus is a big thing with intention, and the belief we have in ourselves supports that.

Laser focus means that you are feeding into the frequency of that intention and inspired thoughts, opportunities and messages come to you quicker and easier when you believe with all of your heart.

Part 4:

NEXT LEVEL INTENTIONS

*First it is an intention. Then a habit.
Then a practice. Then a second nature.
Then it is simply who you are.*

BRENDON BURCHARD

ARE YOU AWARE OF THE POWER IN YOUR INTENTIONS?

One of the most under-rated powers that we all have instant access to is intention. I use it all the time to make huge things happen in my life. I have observed that the block for other people is the fear associated with setting a strong intention. I totally get that but it's important to remember that although an intention requires you to be all in with no guarantee on the outcome, you can still navigate the process without feeling like a failure. Quite often a failed intention shifts you on a path to a bigger and better intention. With that simple shift in perception you no longer need to feel like you are procrastinating in some way, because ultimately you are on a journey, or as I like to call it, an adventure.

To attract what is aligned for you, feel like you already have it, visualise it! However to receive it often requires us to become a higher version of ourselves because we are not fully ready when we set the intention. Powerful intentions are usually big dreams or goals and we have to embark on a journey of self-evolution. That means facing opportunities (challenges) to evolve. I have chatted about my perception of challenges in my other books but it is always worth repeating. Challenges are not brick walls, they are an opportunity to step up into the higher form of ourselves that we need to be to receive our heart's desires and achieve the goals we set. The bigger the goals, the bigger the steps! So yes, it takes courage to reach for the stars but goodness me, what an adventure it is.

Setting an intention energetically sets a powerful current in motion that will ripple to every atom in your body, emitting a force out into the universe that you are often unaware of at the time. That force penetrates the magnetic field and initiates a series of events that when you identify them as being connected to your intentions can lead to a realisation of just how powerful an influence you are on the experiences you have in this lifetime.

Some of the most powerful outcomes I have achieved in my life have been through setting powerful intentions and remaining aware enough to know that the journey to receiving those intentions is not mine to control, but it is mine to navigate. We are the navigators of our own destiny and you can either choose to identify that and have fun making awesome things happen in your life, or you can turn your back on it and never reach the highest version of yourself.

I will talk about aligned intentions versus ego-based endeavours because it is important to identify what is aligned with your highest potential and what is just a selfish pursuit that does not advance us in any way. I have done both many times and I have to say there is nothing like the feeling and rewards that come from being in total alignment with your highest potential. Many people do not get to experience that for themselves in their lifetime and that makes me very sad indeed. So ask yourself the question, 'Have I ever felt truly aligned?' I promise you that you will know if you have.

Setting clear intentions not only relieves us from the stress of uncertainty, it also gifts us focus and clarity.

The three steps of intention success.
1. Set the intention,
2. Connect with the knowing
3. Stay the course. When time and circumstance align, magic happens.

Intention fused with action equals magic.

K P Weaver

THE COLOSSAL POWER OF A LOVING INTENTION

There is a power almighty, and it is closer to your grasp than you could ever imagine. It is simply loving intention!

I am living proof that when you pursue a thought and action it with loving intention you can make ANYTHING happen in your life.

A loving intention can heal the most broken bond, a body that needs regenerating and much more than we can fathom. Why? Because loving intention is the fuel of superheroes; it shines a light into any darkness. The evidence is there in your own life should you choose to see it.

Think about two people in your life who have faced similar challenges, be it health, financial, educational etc. Observe how one with loving support and positive healing intentions came through that challenge faster and healthier than someone with a negative mindset and outside influences. Now think about the person who didn't approach the challenge with self-love and had no support. Did they fall further into a downward spiral? Did they hit rock bottom before they rebuilt? Did they become even more unwell or take longer to heal? Or, have they let the challenge define them instead of empowering them?

There are so many different aspects that can be explored but one thing is certain: loving intention will always prevail.

I encourage us all to interact with loving intention when we can. It can ripple out and touch the lives of so many others. Let love prevail.

I will explore The Law of Love in Book Five of The Alchemy of Life Magic series, but when writing on intention I cannot step around the power of this perfect duo because together they are a match made in Heaven!

When we take a moment to think on each individually, we see the potential. Combined, they are a powerful force in our lives and one I believe we have all felt at some time. So why do they work so well together?

The following from The Happiness Coach, Lori Brant captures it beautifully:

Bringing awareness to your state of BEing before you set your intentions allows you to align yourself with who you really are, fuel the intention with love and create more loving experiences in your life. There are two states of BEing, FEAR and LOVE. Remember, what you put out into the Universe comes back to you multiplied. Intentions set from a state of fear can create more fear compared to intentions that are set from a state of love, which can create more to love.

The secret of change is to focus all of your energy, not on fighting the old but on building the new.

SOCRATES

CHANNELLING INTENTION THROUGH LOVE

There is no more powerful way to make things happen in your life than through loving intention. Have you ever noticed that when people live through their passion and put all of their heart into what they are pursuing, things happen faster than if they set unaligned intentions? This is because a key factor in goals coming to fruition comes from nurturing the seed.

I often use the seed planting analogy when sharing how to make things happen in your life. I am a prolific seed scatterer. I have learned not to talk about each seed as I will seem like a scattered person and super procrastinator. What I do now is share when the seed starts to take hold and pop its shoot out of the ground. A wonderful book that I highly recommend called *INTENTION: How to tap into the most underrated power in the universe to create the life you want* by Andrew Wallace, has validated my theories around intentions being likened to seeds.

For instance, it is not OK to just scatter a seedling of an idea mindlessly onto any ground. To give your seed the best chance of taking hold you must plant it in the right soil. When you set an intention that is aligned with your highest potential, you are going to want to give it the best start by planting the seed of it in the environment in which you want the intention to come to fruition. This is a skill you will learn. I have lots of ideas, all of the time, and some I am sure are million dollar ideas; but I may not have the passion to nurture those seeds to fruition so I scatter them, maybe for someone else to find and grow themselves. The inspired thoughts that grip my soul, the ones I KNOW with all my being are aligned with my highest potential, those seeds I take time to plant. Those are the seeds I have been raking my soil for, the seeds I will go the extra step for to ensure the soil is perfect for them to grow in. Once planted, it's time for the hardest step of all, the unknown!

We can never know what is happening beneath the surface. We may show up every day and water that little seed but we don't know for sure if it has taken hold. Other elements are needed for the seed to really thrive, the warmth of the sun and other things that are often beyond our control. We can mimic them but still it is a blind endeavour filled with hope. By being mindful and knowledgeable about the process and what the seed needs, we can help in some way. And then we wait, we show up for that seed and we wait for as long as it needs to find its way to ground level and peek through the ground. Until that magical moment occurs I keep myself distracted and possibly plant other aligned, inspired thought seeds, because pinning all of your hopes on one seedling is not well advised unless you are confident and have the privilege of dedicating all of your time to that seed to ensure its safe passage through the soil.

When your seed is growing into a flower or even a tree, you will both instinctively and knowledgeably know how to take care of it. As it grows it may need more than you can give so it is important to identify when you need support. Connections are vitally important in successful seed growth, for whether it is a single flower or a full crop, commitment is required to nurture it to fruition.

'One way to ensure an abundant harvest is to create greater connection with ourselves and others.'
Andrew Wallace

One final note about the seed analogy is to be mindful about intention setting. Try to avoid planting your seed in someone else's garden, for they might claim it as their own after you have put all of your loving intention and sweat equity into nurturing it to fruition.

A true intention or belief does not need to be spoken. It is revealed through one's own action.

Owm'r

INTENTION AND FOCUS

There is infinite power in your intentions when you fuel them with focus. This is one of the keys to success! Whenever you are setting an intention, being aware and mindful of what you are giving energy to is very important. What you are thinking of the most is what you are going to attract the most and if you are lucky enough to live life on a high vibration then aligned opportunities will be lining up to present themselves to you. It's important to ensure that when you set the intention, all of your thoughts are positive and aligned with what you want to achieve. *Distracted thoughts get diverted results.*

So, let's explore focus for a moment. I believe there are various levels of focus.

1. Absolute focus
2. Hopeful focus
3. Core Value focus
4. Distracted focus

Let me share with you my definition of each.

- **Absolute focus** is when someone is all in and keeps their intentions close to their mind at all times, ready to pounce on an opportunity at any time. They may even compromise some of their values in the process because the hunger to achieve is so strong.
- **Hopeful focus** is when someone sets an intention but does not apply much focus to it, hoping that it will manifest itself. They hope that it will be handed to them on a plate.
- **Core Value focus** is my favourite. It is when someone sets an intention with absolute focus but aligns any decisions with their core values so that they do not jeopardise their happiness in the pursuit of their goals.
- **Distracted focus** is when someone thinks they want something but deep down they don't because their focus keeps navigating away from the intention they have set. If you have distracted focus when setting intentions, consider two things.
    1. Is it the right time for this intention to happen?
    2. Is this something that you think you want to achieve or something your heart is not in?

I can promise you that when something is truly aligned with your higher purpose you will not get distracted. It will make your heart beat that little bit faster, it will wake you up in the middle of the night with excitement and it will be the best adventure of your life.

I focus most intently when I am producing books. Each project will receive full focus to get it through production and over the line. It is when I don't stop and give full focus at the important times in the schedule that things go wrong. Things that matter to you deserve your full focus.

When I am focused on my personal intentions, I may have a different hat on but I have the same level of commitment. I make sure to check in and focus some high vibrational thoughts on my personal endeavours regularly because they are as important as my professional goals.

There are things that you can leave to the universe that will align when the time is right, but there's a lot of background work that has to happen as well and understanding that is important. Focus will be required so be prepared for that because that's what we sign up to when we set powerful intentions.

It's work that is making something magnificent happen, so that is why focus is important. Your focus will be rewarded, your hard work will be rewarded when it's aligned with your intentions, and you know that because you feel that energetically within yourself. It's actually science! Think about your energy, your atoms, your body, the biology of you and feel that deeply because we're all one, tapped into an electrical current; you will know it and feel it.

If it's energetically aligned with what you're pursuing it will light you up; if it's not, then it's just going to feel like a slug because, you know, that has you going nowhere.

    Focus and set the goals and enjoy the journey of making it all come together.

    What type of focus will you give your intentions?

*It is a precarious undertaking to say
anything reliable about aims and intentions.*

ALBERT EINSTEIN

INTENTION AND CASH FLOW

I believe we all have lessons to learn when it comes to money. It is one of the things I feel is valued way too much in this world when time and even kindness are worth more. I know money can make wonderful things happen in the world but my issue is that the wrong types of people are prioritising money. We need more good people prioritising money in their lives because when good people have money, good things happen!

One of my life lessons is about money. I am an in-one-hand-out-the-other type of person. (Anyone relate?) I set an intention for a million dollar year, and I achieved it. Yes, I made a million dollars in one year, but I also spent one million dollars. Why? Because I see money as potential for growth. If there was a value on the experiences, things I have made happen with that money, then I would be a billionaire. I use money to fuel bigger intentions and sometimes that means waiting. Patience is a virtue I have come to value immensely.

Yes, I may have a forward thinking attitude to money but I am also a good person and through the money I earn, jobs are created, books and stories are shared with the world and I am building the wealth of a press that will hopefully sustain me in my latter years.

Where there is a will there is always a way is one of my life mottos and so when I set an intention and want it enough, then the money needed comes flooding in because I believe it will and I never have any fear around money. Money is a commodity to make things happen, to keep my family living a beautiful life, to give to others so that life can be better for them. Money is good as it can do good things.

Think about your relationship with money. How do you feel about it? Are you in a scarcity or abundant mindset the majority of the time?

Our attitude to money at any given time is reflected in our daily lives and our dominant thoughts.

There are times when I feel like the richest person and there are other times when I am robbing Peter to pay Paul. I don't know if I will ever be different and I don't know if I ever want to be. It makes me feel alive. When I need to manifest money it is a hunger to make something wonderful happen and motivates me to get up and provide value to others so that I can achieve wonderful things for myself and them. Everything I do is through honest to goodness intention to do goodness. And that, I have found, is always rewarded.

One of the biggest lessons we can learn from money is that if we have an abundant mindset when it comes to outgoings and a scarcity mindset when it comes to income then we need to be mindful of that. The person who gives a lot financially will need to fill up the cash reserves. I'm a giver and creator so I struggle with this in the sense of I know what to do and have done it, but enjoy more the creating things from money part more than the saving part. It's kind of like the saying that the money burns a hole in my pocket. I do know that if I won Lotto I would give most of it away, not recklessly but to share more goodness with the world through programs, free resources etc. I would give my most precious commodity of time to others.

One of the elements of money I struggle with is who determines what good practice is when it comes to finances. People say that money makes the world go around, I say love makes the world go around.

I love what money can make happen in my life and in the lives of others. I also realise how lack of money mindset or recklessness through gambling etc can ruin and consume someone's life.

Money is energy so it is important to know what it is for you. What is your money story? Do you host limiting beliefs from your childhood that don't serve you now? Most of us do and that's OK but we can unlearn things in our adulthood and create our own personalised belief system that will serve us better and fuel our dreams.

There is no reason why you can't be the next person to win Lotto. Do you believe you can? Do you even do Lotto? It's all an energy exchange. I often say to the Lotto person, *'I'm going to come in here one day, scan my ticket and the machine will say, your ticket is a winner, would you like to know the amount? And when I click yes it will have a six figure sum there.'* I believe that I have as good a chance as anyone and my part in the energy exchange is to show up, choose my numbers and buy my ticket. Whether the lady behind the counter believes me or not is irrelevant; what is relevant is that I believe it.

One thing I know for sure is that when you think at a higher vibration money flows more easily. I have used *The Secret Money app* to shift my mindset to abundant thinking. The affirmations help eliminate negative money thoughts and I recommend it. Money is energy. When you come to realise this it may overwhelm you at first but once you play around with it and get some traction when you focus on positive money thoughts and frequency, then you will see a dramatic change in your bank balance.

It's important to remember that as money is energy it does require energy to generate it. Be mindful of how much time and what you are willing to compromise to manifest this into your life. It may not be an energy or a side of you that people who love you like to experience. But it is important to remember that to do good things in the world money helps immensely. For example, I used to be able to sustain my life at a much lower cost but as I have raised my vibration and the things I want to achieve then I needed to align with that and raise the cash flow to sustain it. I've had a huge evolutionary process, so much so that in the past five years, my income has increased to ten times what it was to keep my businesses going, which is wonderful.

I'm able to have staff and do all of those high level things I want to do. To sustain that business, every now and again I need to stop relying on my intentions and build up the cash flow bank. When that happens, I go back into doing the work that sustains the business. It is a cycle that I've come to identify and embrace and I use it to align with my values and ensure that I have a work/life balance because that is so important to me.

And of course, this does not just apply to business, it also applies to life. If you want to manifest a holiday, set the intention and work with what that is for you, feel what it is like and be aware of opportunities to make it happen. It might not even be cash, it could be a competition. The main thing is to be aware that when you set the intention, it is in motion so don't block it from coming to you. Your job is to action the thoughts and opportunities that come your way.

My recommendation is if you want something in your life to change, you have to do things differently. Change an aspect of how you are doing something, change perspective.

We all know that when we act instead of react it sets a ball in motion and that is what we want. Super charge your abundant mindset through positive affirmations and maintain a high vibrational thought frequency when you think money!

What are your money ambitions? Do you believe they are achievable? Write down your money intentions for the next year, five years, ten years below.

Part 5:

INTENTION AND QUANTUM ENERGY

Most things have been done,
but they have not been done by you.

Elizabeth Gilbert. Big Magic.

UNIVERSAL THINKING AND INTENTIONS

I was recently gifted the absolute gift of reading *The Universal One* written by Walter Russell. It is complex but I got the essence of it and understood the intricacies of this book that I believe was a game changer when it was released more than 100 years ago. Although quite philosophical, it is all about the oneness of thoughts and matter and how our thoughts create things. I adore this book, the language and deep level thoughts fascinate me. It was a gift from my dear friend and fellow quantum thinker Adrea L Peters, who knew I would 'get it'.

Walter talks of the one God, the Universal One, and how

God is in everything we see and do and is in us also. God is omnipresent! I am talking about the almighty creator who we see as larger than anything but yet can be as small as anything too. Our thoughts create things, our thoughts are part of the omnipresence of God. When we realise that we have access to infinite power closer than we can ever imagine it begins to sink in that when we adjust to universal thinking we can change our reality with a mere thought.

So, let's make this relative to our daily lives. Taking responsibility that our thoughts create things is a pretty big responsibility. I know I have felt it. One thing I have come to realise is that many people pass the responsibility to others, therefore they pass the power over their lives to someone else too. How are we to reach our full potential if we pass the baton to someone else? They are not inside us, they don't know what makes us who we are, or what our soul needs. Only we as individuals will receive that magnificent feeling of knowing that we are on the right track, those beautiful serendipitous moments that come like little sign posts on our journey. For me they are the number 22. It pops up in front of me when I least expect it. Only yesterday I went to an adventure playground with my kids and out of a full box of numbers I could have been given out pops #22. I am mindful of that and it makes me smile every time I see this number. That smile and little glow is universal, it emits from my heart and becomes something lovely.

That is why we need to understand how significant universal thinking is when it comes to intentions. When we set an intention, it is in a process of becoming matter. Thoughts become things! It is a universal law. As philosopher Bob Proctor is well known for saying, *'If you can think it in your mind, you can feel it in your hand.'*

That goes for all thoughts and that is why I encourage everyone to maintain a positive thought vibration as often as possible because thoughts do become things and the universal law does not determine between positive or negative, it provides for all equally.

There are so many intricacies in life, the universe is in harmony with all, everything that we can feel, think and see. The following flowed from me after listening to Jo Dispenza have a conversation about how energy becomes matter. I was not going to keep it in the book but something called for it to stay and so here you go.

This universal law of motion is one of equilibrium from the beginning of a motion to the maximum potential of that motion. During its progression the stability exchanges, and its reality becomes an illusion of stability but is anything ever truly stable? There is a true position for every potential and when that is achieved maximum impact is made. The true position must be found for the exact dimensions of the universe or constant energy which is stored up as mass.

Have you ever thought about how you can really like something and for someone else it will just go over their head? They have no interest whereas to you it is an all-consuming passion. Think of it in terms of setting an intention; their intentions may not be super ambitious whereas yours are. What you pursue lights you up, fuels you and propels you forward and that is all that matters.

A quote you have probably heard me mention on a few occasions is, 'When time and circumstance align, magic happens.' What it means is, do what you can now with what you have and when the time and circumstances align then that is when you will reap the rewards. Patience is gruelling for ambitious people who want everything yesterday.

Whilst writing this paragraph something profound happened to me and it is all aligned with universal thinking and intentions as it was a sign that came after an inspired thought that I am to action. I was driving to Bunbury, south of Perth in Western Australia with my kids at approximately 7am. It is an hour and a half drive on the highway from our home and we were about half-way there. Suddenly I had a very clear inspired thought and a scenario played out in my mind. A thought popped into my head that I should go on my Facebook page to ask if any of my contacts could put me in touch with Oprah or her team. I then had a clear vision of me chatting with her first on a Zoom call and then in a Soul Sunday scenario. It was so clear, so comfortable and I knew it would happen and I would know when it was time.

The message was that we would chat about focus and faith and how it can get us to where we want in life. 'Full focus and Unwavering Faith'. It was one of those magical thoughts that I have had happen and have actioned in my life for magical results. But something next level happened, for a huge eagle flew in front of my windscreen, a couple of feet from my car. Its wings were spread wide, it looked exactly like the image below. For it to happen after my epiphany moment I knew it was a clear sign. So, when I got home, I googled the meaning of seeing a wedge-tailed eagle...

'Universally, eagles are a symbol of power; they can rise over the world, seeing and understanding all. Possessing keen eyesight, they can have a higher perspective on things. They bypass "not seeing the forest for the trees" and can indicate a talent for problem-solving. If a Wedge-tailed Eagle crosses your

path in flight, remember the ability you have in being able to take flight and view your world from a higher perspective, to see the bigger picture. An eagle can see the smallest movement and act quickly. You too can act as soon as you see your goal – don't wait, or your chance, like a startled rabbit, may be gone!'

It blew my mind! Watch this space.

Intend things with passion, intend things with belief, intend things with vision greater than your thinking mind can ever imagine; give it permission to grow into what it needs to become in order for it to be worthy of your intention.

*Intend to be happy and watch
as life smiles back at you.*

K P Weaver

THE SCIENCE OF INTENTIONS

I cannot talk about the science of intention and not mention the amazing Dr Joe Dispenza, and I strongly encourage you to go and check out his videos, his content, even join his monthly club where you can go and listen to him live. He is so giving that he hosts a super affordable monthly group where people have access to him.

I share all of his values and thoughts. So I want to dissect this a little bit, just keep it really simple for you to be able to decipher the information for yourself. I highly recommend his books also.

His book Becoming Supernatural is what I'm going to talk about now. I don't have the validation of scientific evidence behind me that Joe does, but we both sing from the same hymn sheet. I use myself as a test dummy and share my journey so that others can learn. I haven't done many tests. I just adore making the impossible possible. Joe's own journey of healing from being a paraplegic is remarkable, a true miracle. Imagine being unable to move, all that is working is your mind; imagine realising that your mind was powerful enough to heal your body.

Joe has dedicated his life to the science of the mind-body connection and has done much research to support his findings. He walks his talk. When you listen to him speak about how a thought becomes matter and the potential of the energy we create with our minds, you will either run away or open your mind to unlimited potential.

I have always had a pretty open mind but listening to Dr Joe Dispenza has helped me throw the gates wide open.

Getting beyond yourself, getting beyond your limiting beliefs and energy blocks is integral to living to your highest potential.

All people are at their best when they go beyond themselves, when they stop worrying about others, when they stop worrying about themselves, when they stop worrying about materialistic things, when they start to find solutions, when they start to trust and have faith in a higher vibration.

When you take a moment to hang out in this thought frequency, it has a knock-on effect in our energy field which subsequently influences the matter, or in more relative terms the things we make happen in our lives. In a nutshell, it means that the energy you create is having an effect and an influence on your life, your three-dimensional environment and everything you are receiving. And it's funny, whenever you start to hang out more in an energy that you are happy and fit into, it feels like the most natural progression.

When you start to vibrate in this field where energy becomes matter it is there that true change happens. There are no limits. Albert Einstein talks about this, he states that the energy field is the sole governing agency of the particle. That can change how we do life because we understand more deeply how our intentions can become powerful forces in our evolution.

When you understand that if you focus your energy on a positive energy field around yourself, hanging out there and going beyond yourself and into that, it is the sole governing agency of your life. Your reality will be influenced and that will reflect not only to you, but to everyone around you. The energy field we create has an effect on the matter, which is our absolute reality.

Some people enter into that energy through prayer. Some people go into that energy through meditation. Some people are so connected that they have instant access to that energetic alignment, often through their thoughts and emotions and oneness with a higher source.

Miracles happen frequently in these energy fields. And as we know, a miracle is an extraordinary event that is not explained by natural or scientific laws and therefore is attributed to a divine agency. I adore that description. And yes, I'm talking about miracles here in the scientific section of this book.

But when you learn how to scientifically get into the divine agency of the field, that's where the miracles happen. And they don't need to be explained because the matter is affected. Your reality is affected and that is all the evidence you need. The evidence is there. You can't ignore it because you have influenced your energy field. It has had a positive effect or a direct and quick effect on the life that is your reality. There's no questioning that. Amazing people like Dr Joe Dispenza and Bob Proctor are doing research that shows us that miracles happen and they happen very fast.

The only thing that is standing in our way is ourselves. It is scientifically proven because the evidence is there. So, let us embrace it, let there be the miracles in the science, because sometimes we don't need to understand every aspect, we just need to embrace the outcome because it serves us best.

To me, intention drives our thinking towards what we want. It is an arrow to our dream.

ADREA L. PETERS

INTENTION AND OUR THOUGHT FREQUENCY

It's important to think about what happens when we align our intentions with our thoughts. The emotions that are a product of our thoughts are what influences our energy and what and how we attract things through the intentions we set. Therefore it is so important to be mindful of our thoughts because they determine the frequency we put out into our energy field.

It is a metaphysical experience that some people are aware of and others are not. When you set an intention, it's important to be mindful of how you are feeling at the time you set it. If you're feeling high vibrational at that time then go for it, that is a great energy in which to set intentions. One thing is certain in this life, if you think low vibrational thoughts you will experience a low vibrational life. That is all well and good if that is what you choose your life experience to be. As a business owner who lives her life by design, I know the power of high vibrational thinking and how our businesses can thrive and our lives flourish because of it.

So, what is high vibrational thinking?

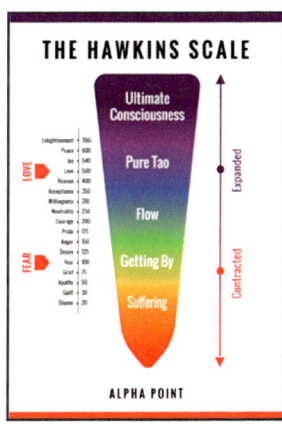

It is simply being mindful of your thoughts and the emotions you feel! Our thoughts determine how we feel and the emotions we feel become energy which is emitted out into our energy field, and that influences our external experiences because it influences how people react to us. Every action causes a reaction! What we put out is what we attract back. It is not gobbledegook, it is science!

When we hang out in the higher vibrational energy scale, we attract bigger results that have a higher percentage success rate. How do I know this? I live it, all the time. I have tested, observed, and shared (probably overshared) my results. I notice that people want to hang out with those who make high vibrational choices because of the effect that occurs when their energy ripples into their life and creates some positive results.

Above is The Hawkins Scale that shares the emotions connected with high vibe living. I choose love, joy and enlightenment as my go to emotions and they serve me well.

Even on a bad day I never really fall any lower than flow. I never go anywhere near fear, and that is because for me there is no fear in *Knowing* and I am a huge advocate that we should reconnect with our natural ability to know.

I suggest you take a moment to look at the diagram and see where you hang out most. This self-awareness can be a powerful insight and with a simple shift in perspective you can change your frequency and your life.

Here are some tips to switch from a low to high vibration quite quickly:

- Be mindful for 21 days to create a new habit of thoughts.
- Practise gratitude.
- Do more of what lights you up.
- Choose you; self-care without any guilt.
- Make time to have fun!
- Get some sleep! When we feel refreshed and recharged, we feel better!
- Surround yourself with people who lift you up.
- Believe that anything is possible.
- Set powerful intentions.

It is not rocket science, but it does take effort and something that some people find hard to do, which is getting to know ourselves so well that we can become the best versions of ourselves, totally in tune with who we are, evolving always and striving to make the most of each day. Life is an adventure, it is to be lived to its fullest. I don't mean in a sense of going skydiving, I mean knowing what it is that lights us up and doing more of that. When we are happy, those who love us will be happy for us, and they also benefit from our high vibration. Win/win is the best scenario for all.

For every pebble dropped into the ocean, ripples occur, as long as you fearlessly toss in those pebbles with humility and gratitude, giving back to the world more than what you take.

KELLY VAN NELSON

THE MIRACULOUS HEALING THROUGH COLLECTIVE INTENTIONS

I want to talk about miracles and the power of collective intentions to make miraculous things happen. Intentions can be set for our wealth, our goals, for all manner of things, but I want to touch on health because ultimately our health is our wealth. Without our health and the health of our family things don't flow. It is hard to get into that energy field of flow where everything just happens when health worries are foremost in our mind.

That brings me to the power of a collective.

I wrote about this in one of my novels, *The Wish Giver*, which featured the host of a circle who brought people together to generate energy to send that collective vibration to someone in a distant location who was in need of healing. The collective healing power was so powerful that it could be felt by the recipient. Yes, I do know that this is really hard for scientists to prove, but you cannot question the results. That's where the miracle in collective intention really demonstrates the intensity of the energy created and the potential that can be achieved through it. So why not embrace the miracle? Why question it when the results are what we want to achieve, especially when improved health is involved?

So let's go with the flow of it and embrace it and not question it. Just have faith in the collective healing power and don't fear an outcome that should instead be celebrated and embraced. It does require that we step beyond ourselves into that quantum realm, that field of energy where anything is possible, including miraculous healing.

The wonderful Lynne McTaggart, author of *The Intention Experiment*, has brought many, many people together online to heal people and recorded the results.

She has proven that when people come together in a collective energy and focus that energy on one specific thought, person or event something that can't be ignored happens. The frequency can actually be picked up on radars. When people come together who are in that quantum field and their attention on their emotions is absolutely aligned then high vibrational miracles happen. It can also happen individually but collectively the vibration can be picked up.

Collectively, that power is miraculous, it is what can

happen because as Einstein taught us, the energy field influences matter. Sickness is matter; it's matter that is within our bodies. It's in the genetics of our bodies and our biology can shift when we focus energy from a healing field to that source and the proof is there. When many people combine their energies together and send it to that source a miracle can happen.

Why do so many people choose not to believe that? In doing that they can block the potential. Why go against that? Why not believe that those miracles happen? There's nothing to lose, only something to gain. I have faith that that is exactly what is happening through that energy, through that high vibrational field beyond ourselves, around where people meet collectively and have a combined energy field. I'm not almighty but I choose to do my bit.

Powerful energy field projects onto matter, onto illness, a cancer or an ailment, a broken heart, anything. When that occurs, miracles happen. Things start to shift within the universe to make things happen. So collectively, we need to think about what we can do within ourselves. What can we make happen collectively that will make miracles happen in our own lives, but also in other people's lives, because that's what will heal our world, that's what will heal our families, and that's what will make a real difference in our world.

I know it may seem intense, but my goodness, if we only knew the power that we have at our disposal the world would be a different place. When we let someone else lead the way we surrender our power instead of standing alongside them to make a difference. We may have different things that are important to us but I'm sure there are plenty of people who have the same interests, passions and values as you that you can connect with and create a super energy that is almighty, powerful and fuelled through love. That is the almightiest power of all because love conquers all. Have you ever felt what it is like to heal something through love? Maybe you haven't been mindful of it but most people heal through opening their hearts to others. In my next book in the series, *The Law of Love*, you learn all about the love and it is an almighty power.

But for now, let's focus on the miracle of the intentions that we can set to make our world and the world as a whole a better place. And can you imagine not giving back, for when you give you ultimately receive. It's not about karma, it's based on science and physics. You receive because you are in the energy of giving, and that energy and the miracles that you are projecting on other people is around you. You are going to benefit from that energetically, but also materially in the reality around you.

How exciting is that! Do we not all want more of that in our lives? I say *yes*. I say *yes* to miracles. I say *yes* to intentions. And I say *yes* to us making a difference in the health and wellbeing of others.

Intend with purpose. Intend with love. Intend with compassion. Intend with integrity. Intend with Knowing. Intend with all your might.

K P Weaver

THE SELF-FULFILLING PROPHECY WHEN YOU LIVE THROUGH THE MIRACLE OF INTENTION

Before I go into this, I want to share with you a definition of Self-fulfilling prophecy:

A self-fulfilling prophecy is the socio-psychological phenomenon of someone 'predicting' or expecting something, and this 'prediction' or expectation coming true simply because the person believes it will and the person's resulting behaviours aligning to fulfil the belief. Wikipedia

When you live through the miracle of intention you can

absolutely predict where you're going to go because you are the person who's in charge just by setting your Intentions, honouring your Knowing and being Mindful of the opportunities that come your way.

These three principles of living a life without fear and on purpose are so powerful that yes, you can have your own self-fulfilling prophecy. You can determine where you're going to go in life simply because you honour the work and the possibility of the miracles that come through your intentions. You're so connected with yourself through your knowing and also you are mindfully aware of the opportunities that are aligned with those intentions. Therefore, there's no risk.

There's no fear. All you need is the courage to move forward and absolutely own your own self, clear in your own self-fulfilling prophecy.

I don't do expectation. Through expectations of others there can often be disappointment, and as I like to live in a high vibration, I don't like the feeling that brings. We cannot rely on others to act or react how we expect them to, we have no right to expect that. So I come from an approach that any goodness that comes from my actions is a bonus. I don't expect anything from anyone else, ever, but I can expect things from myself when I set these intentions; and when I connect with my knowing and when I'm mindful, the results often surpass any of my expectations.

And that is guaranteed because that vibration that I hang out in brings up the goods every time, every single time. So whether you're focusing on achieving something in your business, or a personal goal or something to do with your relationship, you can achieve all of that when you live through the miracle of your intentions and the knowing that's connected to that and being mindful of the opportunities that come your way. And that is so exciting.

Can you imagine the power if everybody knew the potential and what they can do?

Take a moment to think of the possibilities…

Mystical experience!

Where focus goes, energy flows.

TONY ROBBINS

THE SHIFT IN ENERGY WHEN YOU LIVE THROUGH INTENTION

When you live through intention the impact on your life is instant. It does not take long to see things start to shift and align. Not all of it is wonderful but I cannot emphasise enough how important it is to focus on the positive opportunities and inspired thoughts that are being gifted to you.

It is a good time to mention that when we set intentions, the things in our lives that no longer serve us will start to fall away. It's all the ebb and flow of manifesting. We cannot hoard everything, in fact if you are reader of all of my books or part of my social platforms you will hear me talk on the importance of doing a life de-clutter every now and again. For me it is a small de-clutter every three months and a larger cull every year, usually when my children have summer holidays. Working with their calendar works for me because my life by design ensures that I adjust my pace at the end of every school term for two weeks and then a six-week slow down mainly in January. I urge you to find a similar flow that works in your life and just roll with it, committed but not painfully.

People in your world will align with your intentions just as you will align with theirs. To have support around you allows you to maintain magnificence.

Belief is an important principle when it comes to intentions because when you believe that something is possible it energises it, it lifts your energy and you will be present in a higher energy. I always suggest that you take a moment to have faith in the outcome even if you cannot see it right now. Trust that everything is conspiring to bring your intention from a thought vibration into a real life experience.

It is good to be mindful of your energy throughout the manifesting process but also allow it to flow and be exactly what it needs to be. Loving intention is usually a big part of everyone's intentions. If someone wants to manifest a lot of money, they must first believe it is possible and also love the feeling money brings to them. Being mindful of your energy and emotional levels benefits the process immensely. It is when I catch up on sleep, eat well and am happier in my day-to-day life that things flow and my intentions gain traction. This observation is personal, but I do believe it is universal because when we focus on reenergising our body and mind everyone and everything benefits.

So when you set intentions, know the power of your

energy and be mindful to keep your mind, body and soul at its highest level of wellness so that your energy can do its job in making your heart's desires become your reality.

CONCLUSION

Living through intention, when harmonised alongside the other six Life Magic principles, can see you experience life with no limitations.

Your job is to get crystal clear with your intentions so that the universe understands exactly what it is you want to achieve.

Intend through your knowing and you will make unwavering decisions without fear, because there is no room for fear when setting powerful intentions.

My wish for you is that you truly know what it is that you want to achieve in your life.

Intention + purpose + core values = perfect scenario for living to your highest potential without compromise.

Let's face it, there is no point in achieving your heart's desire if you have to compromise your core values. It will never feel worth it or aligned with your highest potential.

Always be mindful that when you set intentions and pursue them with loving intention, you will experience higher yielding results and the journey will be so much more enjoyable.

We are divine humans with capabilities beyond our wildest dreams. I hope that by reading *The Miracle of Intent* you have been able to unlock some blocks that may have been holding you back from living your best life.

We all are worthy of living the life of our dreams and only you know what it is that you truly want. So instead of looking outward for validation, look inward for guidance because our internal compass navigates and serves only us, no one else. It has our truest intentions as its highest priority. Ask and you will receive, your genie is awaiting!

GUEST INTENTION STORIES

Intention fuels flow.

Five steps of intent to turn dreams to reality
By Kelly Van Nelson

BAG it

As a young girl, I dreamt of working in an office to save enough money to carve a better life for myself, eventually enabling me to live overseas. To me, this was crazy ambitious, given I lived in a working-class area dogged with unemployment and crime. Securing a job in a good environment was a huge flag on the hill. My father passed away in his forties, my mum, from whom I am estranged, remarried multiple times, and home was a council house in the inner-city concrete jungle of Newcastle-upon-Tyne. School was also a place where I was bullied relentlessly over a long period of time. I left high school at sixteen, unable to afford university, but I was bright and knew I could apply myself to any task in front of me. Not long after leaving, I bought a one-way bus ticket to London, found myself that elusive office job, and became fully self-sufficient, enough to be able to fund a night school education that earned me a distinction in computer studies.

On top of this unwavering desire to stand on my own two feet, which was fuelled by basic survival instincts, there was another big audacious goal (BAG) I carried with me everywhere; I wanted to be an author. My two best friends recall times during our high school years when I openly stated my intent to one day write a book. Reading and writing were my mechanisms to escape reality. Everybody has a story inside of them, fact or fiction. I just had an overwhelming desire to capture mine on paper. Writing was and always will be my therapy, a way to recharge my batteries and replenish the soul by channelling negativity from life's challenges and turning it into positive energy.

Today, I work full time as Managing Director of a global Fortune 500 company, sitting on the executive board of the Australian business. The role is my dream office job in the staffing and HR solutions space, putting people into work every day. It is extremely demanding, with a large team spread across eighteen locations, but it is fulfilling on so many levels. My books are on retail shelves globally, my short stories and fiction have made it into numerous publications internationally, and I have a number one bestselling poetry book that won the Roar Success Gold Award for Best Book and was gifted to Oscar winners and Hollywood celebrities. I'm also married to my soulmate and have two beautiful children. I've achieved my two childhood goals and continue to set myself new ones.

Don't be afraid to load up life with a couple of BAGs.

Unpack Your Luggage

At some point, you need to pause and unpack your BAGs, otherwise the weight of carrying those dreams on your shoulders can become heavy. Assess what is in there and what you can practically do to turn those dreams into reality. Restate your intent to yourself and others. My intent was to write a book. Simple. But if I left that intent locked in my luggage forever, it would be damn tiring. So, I began to take small action-oriented steps towardss achieving that goal. I started writing poems and short stories, submitting them to competitions, and began writing a novel. Rejection letters began to make their way into my post box. Then I landed a small win. My first poem got published in the UK. I wrote more pieces. Got a few more credits to my name. Finished the novel which placed in a bigger literary competition for unpublished manuscripts. That generated enough interest to get an agent to take me on. I found an amazing publisher willing to take me under their wing. Wrote five books, a mix of poetry and fiction. This took a decade of hard work to achieve, done by constantly adding building blocks built on a foundation of unwavering resilience. Small steps. Big Audacious Goal achieved.

Be action oriented. A dream without action will always remain a dream.

Front Up

To set out on a journey of intent can be daunting but taking baby steps towards achieving a big audacious goal means ongoing achievements along the way help to drive enough momentum to keep the hard work sustainable for the long haul. No road is ever smooth. I have a spreadsheet a mile long filled with information on rejections I've received. What is important is to not be blocked by these bumps. I look at each one, allowing myself a day or so of sitting on that hard stone, pondering, chewing on the feedback, thinking about what I can do better next time. Then I either walk around that rock, push it to one side, or climb over the damn thing. If you sit on a boulder forever, that becomes the end destination, so it is important to front up to challenges and take that next step again. If we accept curve balls are par for the course, it becomes easier to learn from rejections or mistakes and embrace new ideas or opportunities. Make the decision to front up and move ahead or be happy with the view of that rock.

<u>Create Ripples</u>
With hard work comes reward. Moments of euphoria from successfully kicking goals, from believing the impossible is possible and backing this up with an action plan. I choose to celebrate these wins personally, with family or friends, but also do so publicly, using social media to generate more positive energy, giving back to others wherever I can. This might be through something as easy as sharing a few insights on areas of expertise or introducing someone to a contact in my network, but it can be with an even greater purpose too, by involving myself in forums that generate conversation about issues that matter. These are typically the passionate social issue topics I write about, such as anti-bullying, domestic violence prevention, and mental health awareness. Celebrations of success become more widely spread, networks get bigger with reciprocal introductions, useful insights get shared back to me, changes happen for the better. For every pebble dropped into the ocean, ripples occur, as long as you fearlessly toss in those pebbles with humility and gratitude, giving back to the world more than what you take.

Embrace Authenticity

People often ask how I manage to juggle being a mum, a full-time corporate worker, and a successful author. At first, I found myself dancing around this conundrum. I'd never allowed myself a breather to look at the big picture around the direction life had taken. Yet this question played on my mind, challenging me to stop and think about how I was managing so many moving parts. I realised my life was hurtling along, compartmentalised into three parallel worlds, all competing for time, energy, and my full attention. Family. Work. Writing. It was mentally taxing, so I sought out a mentor who helped me embrace new ways that allowed my authentic self to shine through in all corners of life. The result is a new blended approach to living a well-rounded life, thriving with purpose and intent. I took my daughter into my new Sydney office to meet some of the team and engaged with my son's school to participate in a career fair, sharing insights with two hats on, as both an author and a corporate executive. My children are now my biggest supporters at various literary events as well as my toughest critics. I spoke publicly to colleagues on National Anti-bullying Day about the power of resilience during my tough childhood and the importance of mutual respect in the workplace. I had always tried to front up as Superwoman to mask the imposter syndrome feeling of never being good enough, so being more vulnerable like this with colleagues about deeply personal issues was alien and incredibly difficult at first. It felt like I was baring my soul to people who had never seen that introspective side of me before. But it was also liberating to let the barriers down. I could be a mum, business leader and a writer all at once. No more jumping between multiple personas. Now I've merged my parallel worlds into one universe where I have way more space to be just me, one whole and authentic person.

I encourage others to embrace everything you do with absolute, unwavering, authenticity. You don't have to be Superwoman. Just be you. It's enough.

Adrea L Peters

As the ideas for *Becoming Truitt Skye* flooded into me, I swallowed them whole. Each new idea sparked another need for research, and then more ideas. The idea flooding has yet to end. I couldn't get enough soul knowledge. Mind you, this was circa 1996, so the world we now know of self-help and inner exploration rarely included the word soul. Yet I was addicted. I would not stop until I got it right. Or right enough for a transformational piece of fiction.

Intention One:
My dream was always to change the way we see death.

Because I needed to see that nothing ever ends.

I've experienced a bucket load of goodbyes. Deaths of dear friends, including the boy who gave me my first kiss, and the one who got away—because he died. I have mourned young friends who traversed this extraordinary planet for less than two decades and died from multiple sclerosis, cancer, car accidents, and suicide. I said goodbye to my first best friend, my beloved granddaddy, mere days before my first day of high school. My grandmothers, Katie and Thea, still linger strong making sure I am getting on with this one precious life. My dad lives so strong within me that despite the fact that he left a couple of years back, I talk to him more than ever. He's peering over my shoulder right now reminding me it's OK to cry big elephant tears when I think about my granddaddy. "He loved you too," he whispers. "We all do."

I researched death with vigour, reading texts from Kubler-Ross to Sagan. I listened to endless lectures from Caroline Myss on the anatomy of the soul, energy, chakras, angels and trees of life. I dove into Buddhist philosophy and metaphysics. Always with the same question: What actually happens when we die? Where exactly do we go? Of course, no one has the answer. They claim to be experts with a variety of degrees, but they haven't died and come back to tell us about it.

Or have they?

That question got me a little fixated on time. And Albert Einstein. And Alan Lightman and his teacher, Richard Feynman. Physicists seemed as obsessed as I was about explaining things. I *needed* to know how time worked. Was death actually "the end"? Of what? Again, where did we go? We could not possibly end. I did eventually dabble with Abraham-Hicks, Wayne Dyer, Louise Hay and a handful of others, but it was the science, specifically the quantum mechanics, the science of endless possibilities, that took its hold on me and helped me see that *everything* is true. Choice, observation, perception, those were the keys.

Deciding was the only thing that mattered.

We *get* what we think about.

To me, intention drives our thinking towards what we want. It is an arrow to our dream. When we intend, we receive our dreams. When we think without aim, without intention, we still get what we think about, but it may not be what we want. May as well amp our thinking into intending, hey?

***

Once I had my concept for Truitt—this smattering of what happens when we die and how it relates to living with intention, I was off and running. It took years to research and write Truitt and I wouldn't have it any other way. Well, I might've but if you were to ask my prior self if the timing was right, she would say, "Abso-freaking-lutely." Each intention needed time to germinate before it took form.

Prior to and during Truitt, I wrote articles for magazines and I wrote several screenplays that received a stack of rejections. So many rejections that I quit sending the query letters out. And I wrote a memoir in letters and photographs that also got rejected many, many times. Each rejection devastated me. And drove me to learn more. That's why I began studying novels. They seemed to cover the full story of story. I wanted to get it right but didn't know boo.

I got a book, *The Weekend Novelist*, and pored through it, doing every exercise, mapping things out as instructed, and drafting pages. But there was no one to give me feedback. No place to take my story. I wasn't learning. I needed more mentoring. I couldn't do it alone. Feedback, whilst rough to receive in those early years of my writing life, was pivotal.

Intention Two:
Get help. Get smarter. Learn more.

My first mentor was a love. An absolute genius who was thoroughly supportive as a teacher. As I tapped out on what I could learn from him, I asked him for a recommendation for a grad school program. I know there isn't a need to get their graduate degree, but it was quite important to me. I wanted a Masters. He sent me to a wonderful school, Seton Hill University, where I wrote the first draft of *Becoming Truitt Skye*. It was a completely different novel than the one that was published, but the gist remains.

Problem was I was too chicken to share my research and knowledge of science in the first three drafts of Truitt. I was scared to use the word soul, much less try to relate it to quantum physics. Life after death novels were not popular. Publishers wanted sappy tales of how hard it is to move on after death. I couldn't write what I didn't believe.

And so I sought feedback: a teacher. At a conference in the middle of nowhere Guatemala, I met a publisher from Penguin, who I so very desperately wanted to buy Truitt. He did not. However, he told me to include my science! Include my incredible knowledge! He helped me map out the earliest plan for the Truitt on shelves now. He told me to take my time. It was my masterpiece. I remember him saying it might take a decade, and it did.

Intention Three:
Include my genius in everything I write.

I am not saying I am a genius. We all have a genius within us. May we share it. May we always include it. May we shine bright and beam our genius in all directions.

After connecting so profoundly with Francesco, I set two new intentions immediately. (To say he changed my life simply does not cut it. There will never be enough gratitude from me to him.)

Intention Four:
To have my literary agent, who will sell Truitt, be a "best friend".

Intention Five:
To partner with a publisher, as equals, completely in it together.

My dears, those are not small. They were mammoth, unheard of, intentions.

And both came true.

Hilariously enough, I found my agent whilst begrudgingly flipping through a magazine to find images for a Vision Board. I was not a vision board kind of gal at the time, but obviously now I am. On a page of Lisa Messenger's *Collective Hub* magazine, was a teeny circle with a photo of a beautiful woman called Anjanette in it. A literary coach and agent in Australia. I cut her out and put her on my board. A few days later I wrote her a long note asking her to consider coaching me through a new draft of Truitt. I wasn't about to pitch yet. Remember, I intended to have a BFF, not merely an agent. Was I conscious of this? Nope.

Once I set an intention, it's free. Better put, I am free. Free to create. Free to express myself fully. Free to get on with it. After all, it's what I intend. May as well ride the wave, or waves, to it.

I asked Anj to please *not* say yes if she did not connect with Truitt. That was a HUGE risk for me to take at that time. Finally I owned my genius. I was desperate for her help and I knew in my bones, she was the one, but I needed her to know it. It didn't matter that I loved Truitt. It mattered that she did. When I heard back from her a few days later, it was magic. Not only did she get Truitt even more than me on some levels, she got me. She saw me. She heard me, and she wanted to help me.

While Anj no longer represents authors, including me, and we remain beautiful friends—which is ALL that ever mattered to me, I am forever grateful to her. She taught me. She guided me. She gave me the gift of support I needed to gain confidence as a writer. With that confidence fully emerging, I've set the intention for my next agent.

The greatest part about having an agent is that they get the rejections, not me. This is nice. Anj revealed to me a year or two in that it was as painful for her as it was for me. I asked her to only tell me when we get a yes, or if she thinks Truitt needs something changed. It only takes the right yes. We had options. We weren't desperate. We could always self-publish. This gave us leverage to find a partner. I was strong, loves, in my intention for a partner as a publisher. I was not going to write one or two books. This was my future. This was my dream. Not something I would take lightly. I hope you don't take your dreams lightly either. They are the matter of you. They are everything.

Anj tried to sell Truitt for years. Yes. Years. Plural. I admit that I was nearing my limit. I did consider quitting. Oh. Yes. I've quit being a writer many times. When I returned from that trip to Guatemala, I didn't write for months. When my screenplays were rejected, and my memoir, I think I quit writing for a year or more. That was before I realised the power of an intention.

Intentions are a big deal.

Can't go back once they are set.

Try as we might, they remain in flight. They don't quit you. Ever. They have patience, even when you don't.

As Karen always says, "When time and circumstances align, magic happens."

She could not be more right. I trust that now. I didn't before I met her.

Eager to get that publishing deal, I headed to a conference in the UK led by my dear friend, Michelle. We were there to Uplift and Uplevel ourselves and each other. She's an energy "editor" who utilises kinetic energy and intention to free us from our limitations. Magic, right? Not so much for me. I felt like a fraud. Everyone in the workshop was experiencing shifts and breakthroughs and meltdowns. I was sipping tea and giggling, but not quite breaking through jack-diddly. And could not understand just exactly where my book deal was exactly. I was aligned with my desire, was I not?

Sitting in the Dublin airport at the gate for my flight home to America, I had a full-on blubbering, red-splotching face meltdown. There was nothing mild about it. This was excellent. Unbeknownst to me at the time, I was on the verge of that book deal. Thing was, along the way, I'd forgotten to set a really massive intention.

Intention Six:
To believe I could live the life of my dreams.

It wasn't until I confessed to Michelle that I didn't know how to be anything else but a writer that I could finally relax and release my fear and doubt. Once I knew it was too late to quit, that I couldn't quit, I settled into waiting as long as it took for my dream to arrive. What else would I do? I *was* a writer. And it was okay for me to dream big, be published the way I wanted to be published, and get on with living the life of my dreams.

Within two weeks, I was talking to Karen on our first of now many video calls. It was magic from the get go. We barely had to speak, it seemed. It was right. She was, and is, a partner with me. A few weeks later, she invited me to invest in her publishing company and become a shareholder. I accepted without hesitation.

Postscript: Anj and Karen had already spoken and Anj knew Karen was going to offer me a deal (Probably during that dang workshop with Michelle!), but Anj wanted me to hear it from Karen firsthand. Of course she did. Because that's what friends do. They want you to feel the magic and the elation. They want you to shine.

Six months later, I sat at that same gate in the Dublin airport after attending the Serenity Press Retreat hosted by Karen at Crom Castle in Northern Ireland. I was soon to hold *Becoming Truitt Skye Book 1: The City on the Sea*.

Intentions flew all over the place. The look and feel of Truitt in the hands of her beloved readers. I intended it to melt into their hands, hearts, souls. I intended to receive positive, inspired, incredible, fun, and personal reactions to Truitt. I intended more Truitt books. More Truitt period in all forms and function. ***Because I know now, for sure, that nothing ever ends.***

Gary Doherty

I'm very much into the universal laws because I believe that I've been vibrating at a level where I'm attracting a whole lot more than I ever have before. I've got so much abundance in my life, and not only financial, it's happening in all areas. My health, my friendships, my network, my business, my confidence, business interests that I'm involved in, things that I've been asked to do, collaborations that are coming thick and fast at me, not the other way round.

It feels amazing. I feel like that's why 2020 has been the most productive year of my life, despite everything that's been going on in the world. I believe that I am on the crest of a wave. I believe I'm in that flow state, and I am going to capitalise on all areas of my life, for the greater good of Think Network. Everybody that's involved, everybody that I'm in contact with, everybody that I collaborate with, everybody that supports me, and we're just in a really good moment, and have been for some time, and we will be for some time.

I have had a very inquisitive mindset in my adult life, not

so much when I was younger. I had less confidence, and I didn't flourish as a human being, I suppose, until my mid-20s, maybe. I had a very influential mentor in my life, Marshall McCollum, and he lit a fire in me, and that's been burning ever since and getting bigger, and will continue to. I have had various different roles, always knew that I had something else to offer, but didn't know what it was, didn't know what my purpose was. It took me 42 years to find my purpose, and I found it, and I'm here now.

Not only that, when I found my purpose, I then investigated why it was my purpose. A lot of people, when they find something they're passionate about, they just roll with it. I actually wanted to know more. I wanted to know why. *Why is this actually something I want to do? Why do I want to empower the world? Why do I want to be a positive change in the world? What's wrong with just doing it in Limavady?* And I wanted to know why I was feeling like this, and why I was enjoying these good things that were happening, and all this buzz that was going on, and the movement that was happening, and the bums coming under my knife. I wanted to know why, and that's a really important part.

I've been so intent on driving on, and I've had affiliation with the world famous global empowerment platform TED. I started my own business, Think Network, which is a more commercial version of TED, but with the same essence. But about two years ago, I was doing a lot of charity work, and I was doing bits and bobs, and I knew that part of my purpose was to serve others. I always knew that. And then I started to find my passions and motivational speaking, and I thought, wouldn't that be amazing to live my life through that lens. I was looking at the TED platform and thinking, I would love to be affiliated with that platform.

In 1986, TED brought out TEDx, and the X stands for independently organised events. People spent a fortune to speak on the stage, and I spent a fortune to sit in the audience to listen to the person that spent a fortune to be on the stage. And TED realised, through a guy called Chris Anderson that they needed to embrace communities. They needed to touch everybody in the world, and they brought out TEDx. And TEDx is a licence-held event, independently organised, and I thought, I want to host one of them.

I researched it, and there had never, ever been one in my city, Derry Londonderry. So I did some more research and I winged in an application. Six weeks later: 'Dear Gary, thank you for your interest in the platform. We've had a quick look at your application, and have decided that it's not fit for purpose. You haven't been granted your licence. Thank you for your interest in TED. We hope you enjoy our content as much as we do.' I wasn't surprised I was turned down, and rightfully so. I hadn't given the platform the respect it deserved, with the preparation in the application that it deserved.

Me being me, the attributes that God has blessed me with are persistence, desire, commitment, and thank God for that. Zero talent, but I was firm in my intention. This was like a high type B stroke type C goal. But when it's never been done before, and there's no pathway, and there's nobody to give you counsel, and there's nobody to tell you how they've done it before, and there's nobody to show you the way, that's type C stuff for me, regardless of an application form. Anybody can fill it out, not everybody can get it.

I took my time with the second application, maybe took about a month to plan it. I was about seven out of ten confident that I would get a positive result. At this stage, I was still a bit of a TED novice, in terms of their expectation levels. Six weeks later: 'Dear Gary, We have reviewed your application, and we are sorry to tell you that it hasn't been successful. Thank you for your interest in the TED platform. We hope you enjoy our content as much as we do.' I thought, OK, that's a kick in the teeth. But again, desire, persistence, commitment. It comes back to your why and how much you want it. I wanted it. Honestly, I can hand on heart say publicly that I knew in my heart of hearts that I wanted it like nobody ever in 26 years that had applied for Derry. And there had been many people applied for it, by the way. It's not as if it hadn't been applied for before. Many people had applied for it, but they couldn't even agree on the name, Derry being a sort of hot potato maybe, through troubles and stuff. Nobody wanted it called TED Derry. Nobody wanted it to be called TEDx Londonderry, and I said, 'I'll call it both. We'll embrace everybody, all sides of the community, no matter who you are and what you are, this is for you.' And I think that blew them away, as basic and all as that sounds.

I went away, and I volunteered at TED events. I attended more TED events. I even got myself to a stage where I was asked to be a judge for the next TED speaker at a local event. I was now Mr TED, locally. I use a phase, 'All in'. You're either all in or forget about it. I'm not interested in half measures for anything, and that applies to life. That's me in life, whether that be health and fitness, training, whatever it is, I'm all the way in, or I'm not doing it, because I just can't be half arsed with anything. It has to be the whole way.

The third application went in, and I thought right, my good Lord, I'm bound to have learnt a lot of lessons here now. Even the language you use in your application is critiqued, the wording is critiqued, the theme that you pick is critiqued, the speakers you anticipate using are critiqued. The perspective that you're coming from is critiqued. Everything is under a microscope, but I felt ready to be under that microscope now. I thought, I have to get this. Interestingly, six weeks took me up to Christmas Eve of 2019. And would you believe it, they took the full six weeks and on Christmas Eve, I got the unwanted gift: 'Dear Gary, We have reviewed your application. You've been unsuccessful on this occasion. We just would like placed on the record our appreciation of your continued enthusiasm for the platform, and we hope you enjoy the content as much as we do.'

I felt defeated in that moment. A lot of people think when somebody achieves great success, or an achievement, and they see the tip of the iceberg, they don't see the 90% of it underwater and struggling. People don't see the struggle. You can imagine what my Christmas was like mentally, for me. And I felt deflated. I felt, for the first time, I could be defeated here. I felt like giving up and I shared those thoughts with some people in a group that I'm in, TIR group. I was reading *Think And Grow Rich* at the time as well, and I came across the story about the three feet from gold. The guy mining for gold gives up, sells the machinery to a scrap man, who then keeps mining for a few feet, strikes gold and changes his life. I was actually reading that story at that time, and I was sharing my innermost thoughts about giving up, and most people were saying, 'You don't need it, Gary, you don't need that. Why do you want it? Give up, forget about it.' Even people that should know better were encouraging me to give up, and I'm talking about influential people that knew what it meant to me.

When your desire, and your vision, and your mission and purpose are so, so, so great, don't give up, find another way. Change the plan. Improvise, adapt and overcome. Do not give up. That is the worst advice anybody can give you. What people should have been doing was giving me scenarios, saying well, what if this? What about that? Not telling me to give up. You should give advice, but you should never tell somebody to leave a marriage, for example, unless of course for their safety. I took that personally. People were giving me this advice to walk away, and I thought, you've just lit the fire again, thanks.

The fire never went out, but it was simmering. I was wavering. I was feeling down, but I wasn't out. Interestingly, I had a big event to focus on, Think Resilience on 30th January and Brian Kennedy was the speaker. So I had four weeks to focus my energy on something that I needed to nail, and we did. We sold 340 tickets, a fully packed out, sold event, and the ripples and waves after that are still being talked about, and it was an amazing event.

One week after that event, I thought, right, I'm going back there again, and this time I'm coming back with a vengeance. This time there will be no reason, zero reason they can tell me I haven't got this licence. And I even said that in my application form in a note. I just said, 'I expect an approval for this licence, after everything that I have done, my commitment to the platform.' I just told them. There is nobody better placed in Derry, or Northern Ireland, or the globe to deliver a TED event than me, nobody anywhere, not alive, that's how passionate I am about it. That's how all in I am about it. I wasn't stopping three feet from gold. That was my gold, and I wasn't stopping for anybody, nobody, not even TED themselves. I actually said to them in the application, 'You would just do as well giving me the licence, because I'm coming back a fifth time, a sixth time, and a seventh time.' And I meant it, I was, and I would have, and I put in the application.

This time I wasn't so sure, because of the three failures, which were only temporary failures. But I put in the application, and I worked out the six weeks. I was moving towards that date with hopeful optimism, because the whole journey before that, that whole year and a half or whatever it was, I was away. I'm a big visualisation practitioner. I don't just visualise it, I get into the emotion of it. I feel it. The hairs on my arms stand. I've got myself into an emotional state before, being so emotionally attached to a type C goal. That's why I make type C goals happen, because I am so, so attached to them, and then you manifest them, because your vibration's so high and you're attracting them, with massive action thrown in. And without fear of public failure, because you need to have the courage to tell other people you believe, and my determination paid off.

On March 6th in Lusty Beg, Enniskillen, I was out for a meal with friends and family. It was a week before lockdown. Nina, the social media manager had invited me down to check out the place. I had never been and she said, 'Why don't you come down? I'll look after you.' We went down, and we stayed in the most beautiful big log cabin. We went up for dinner and at 6:32 (I have it screenshot), sitting, just ready for my meal to come down, the email comes through from TED. It said something like, 'Dear Gary. We are delighted to tell you that you have been awarded the prestigious TEDx Derry Londonderry licence. We thank you for your persistence, and commitment, and enthusiasm to the brand, and we feel there is nobody better than you to deliver that event in that city, and thank you for persevering with it.'

I can't tell you the feeling that came over my body. Unless you're a dream chaser like me, most people won't get that. They won't understand what that meant to me. But I was tearful. I recorded a few videos because I wanted to document the feeling there and then. The rest is history! On January 29th, 2021, we delivered a truly historic event. TEDx Derry Londonderry, a first forever, legacy event. Showtime, the lights, camera, action time. The time when all of the hard work paid off, the fun time.

Emma Weaver

Setting goals and dreams are all part of life's journey, many of us do this regularly. Setting intentions however is a different matter entirely.

This is a much more powerful process, one where you have to feel all the feels and be guided by this. It is imperative that you listen to your inner guide and act on inspired thoughts.

Setting intentions is stating what you intend to accomplish through your actions and the universe providing for you. The key is to be open to receive the help or gentle pull to focus in the moment and be committed to the journey. Know who you are, what you want and why you want it.

Life has a strange way of sending you down a path that you never anticipated. I am the second born to a family of six. I was a studious type, I didn't love school nor did I hate it. I fell in love at a young age and was excited for my future, university, a career and financial stability and a happy life.

Things however did not turn out as I had planned. I got pregnant young and left school after my final year. This was not how it was meant to be, how had I let this happen? Where had my future gone? I felt helpless, the stigma attached to the situation I had just found myself in was cruel and limiting my potential or chances of building a meaningful life.

My beautiful baby girl arrived safely, all 7lb 7ozs of her on a beautiful spring morning. Like every new mum the feelings of love and emotions were there even at my tender young age. I knew I had to do better for my daughter and create change in a society that makes young couples, women or men feel the way I had been made to feel by the cruel judgments that had been made. It is no crime to have a child, no matter what your age.

It was there in that moment I set the intention to finish my education and pave a career, all whilst being a mum and trying to do right by my little family, just the three of us. I didn't know how I was going to do it, I just knew if I set the intention it would happen. The odds were against me, opinions were that now I had a baby that was it, my life was ruined. This was not the end for me, in fact it was just the beginning. With a new perspective on life and a beautiful baby girl to motivate me I honoured my intention.

I enjoyed being a mum, what a gift that many take for granted. I was so grateful how being a mum changed and shaped me even at a young age. I was very independent and set up home for my little family, all the while thinking about my future, setting a good example for my daughter and creating a new way for us. Young mums don't go to college. I felt the whispers of *who does she think she is even having a dream*? It was as if I should hide myself away with my baby. Small minds and judgmental people were not going to deter me.

Coming from a rural county in Ireland I couldn't drive so

this reduced what I could access. We didn't have a lot of money although my partner worked and we surely didn't have enough to fund my aspirations. The intention was there and I trusted it would happen without knowing how. I focused on being a good mum and learning as much as I could from other mums, my mum, health workers and set the foundation to ensure my little girl had the best start in life and all the love she needed.

I was up visiting my mum one day with my little girl when the health visitor called up. She asked me what I was doing and I said, "Nothing at the moment except being a mum." She was happy with my little girl's progress and asked what I had thought I was going to do when I was at school. I laughed nervously as if I should not ever speak of my previous ambitions. We had a long chat and discussed my academic abilities and I told her about my intention to go back into education and create a life for us and show my daughter that even through adversity and challenges we can thrive. There, I had said it, it was now out there and it felt good to tell someone. I felt a mixture of feelings but decided I would own it and it was mine to own.

Two weeks later I was at home with my daughter when a knock came to the door and it was the health visitor. I had not been expecting her. She came in and said that she could not get me out of her head. She had been to the local college and discussed me with student support and got an application form and prospectus to discuss my options. I could not believe it, her belief in me was humbling and I was grateful, however I did not feel ready. I could not drive, we couldn't finance any studies and I was not ready to leave my little girl. We discussed all of my concerns and fears that appeared to be a block for even though my intention was clear I was not actioning it.

There was a bus that could take me directly to college, I could do the course part time and finance was available. All I needed was to be brave and take action and dispel all of those self-limiting beliefs that this could not be done.

Just like that we filled in the form and posted my course application to the college.

The intention had been set. Barriers were there however they could be overcome with action and bravery. Now let's see if I could do this...

I went for an interview and took time to walk around the college and feel what it would be like to attend. It was a tall building in the largest town in the county. The bus depot was not too far away and I was familiar with the town already. I felt tingles of excitement that my dreams could become a reality and that me, a young mum, could proceed with education despite all the obstacles.

The letter came within a week saying that I had a place on the course which was held on a Tuesday every week from 9.15am to 4pm. I would need a placement once a week also. That was it, I had go on, this was the beginning of the next phase of my education journey. I was grateful that I had support to do this and child care was available.

Leaving my little girl was hard, I just wanted to be with her all of the time, however I recognised that completing this course would open so many doors for us and allow me to secure meaningful employment and create a better life.

Everything was in place and ready for me to start, I just had to show up. That's the thing when you set intentions, they need action and for you to show up even when there is fear involved.

A lot happens in four years, I had to keep my head up

and not be deterred from my vision. My little girl grew so wonderfully and to be honest we grew together. I turned eighteen and twenty-one in those years and juggled motherhood and studies. The struggle was real and on many occasions I did not know how I would get through, I just knew I had to.

I became a single mum when my relationship broke down, then tragedy struck and my little girl's dad was fatally injured in a motorbike accident. I was left with sole responsibility for her life, wellbeing, every aspect of her being and that was more motivation to ensure I succeeded.

There were many occasion when things got tough and during those times it was important for me to touch base with why I had decided to embark on this journey; all the influences and factors that had contributed in me getting this far, all of the inspired actions that I had taken and others all aligned with my vision after the intention was set. I trusted the process and grew personally as well as professionally, making my way through college and holding a part-time job.

My little girl was at school now, she had to face one of the biggest hurdles in her life, losing a parent and I needed to step up.

I stood firm in my belief that I could achieve what I had said I would when my little girl was born.

Then on September 11th 2001, a date no one will ever forget due to world events, I graduated with my little girl by my side. I had created what I had said I would, I had followed through and created a new way for us. Nineteen years later this is still the case and my little girl has grown into a beautiful successful woman completing her doctorate as I type this...

I believe when you set an intention and truly believe in it and trust the process, anything is possible. You need unwavering faith that the universe will provide as it did for me.

Peace Mitchell

My eyes were puffy and red from crying in the cramped and cold hotel bathroom. My children were asleep in the room outside and I had nowhere else to go. It had been my dream to do a TED talk for as long as I could remember and yet at the first rehearsal, with the harsh fluorescent lighting, the suffocating rows of desks and chairs and the unfamiliar faces, I had frozen and been unable to speak. I couldn't even give a summary of my topic. I'd left my first draft at home and couldn't remember what I had written or the message I wanted to get across. Although I had written 3000 words it was only the first draft and nothing like the perfectly crafted, well-rehearsed and beautiful final speech that I had imagined myself giving. I wasn't ready. The speaker coach was a fan of improvisation and had given us five minutes to rewrite an 18- minute speech into a three-minute one and played jarring, jaunty music to help motivate us along with the task. I couldn't concentrate, I couldn't remember my speech and I made three poor attempts at recalling it before finally giving up with a page of crossed out incoherent scribble in front of me. As each of the other speakers went up to the front of the room and delivered strong and confident presentations I became more and more embarrassed and wished that the ground would open up and swallow me.

The coach was trying to be helpful. "Come on just give it a go, you have to know what your topic is," she encouraged, but the more she tried to get me to come up to the front of the room, improvise and just give it a go, the more I insisted that I wasn't ready and refused to leave my seat. The walls started to feel like they were closing in and I couldn't get out of there fast enough. It was late by now and I practically ran down the stairs into the dark carpark and drove off feeling hot with shame. I felt like a fraud and a failure. This was supposed to be my dream but now all I wanted was to quit.

Why am I telling you this story? Because following your dreams is hard. It always looks easy from the outside. People rarely tell you the pain and heartache of what it takes to make it happen behind the scenes but I can guarantee it's there. No matter how easy and effortless people make it look or how successful they are, there are always challenges and obstacles to overcome, fear, self-doubt, and second guessing. And without a strong and clear intention for what you want to achieve many people simply give up.

I'd set the intention to give a TED talk four years ago. I'd probably come up with the idea of it sometime before that, but I remember voicing it and telling the world this dream when we first launched the Women's Business School Ignite program, a course designed to inspire women to follow their dreams as entrepreneurs. In my presentation I talked about identifying your superpowers and my example was public speaking. Then I would encourage the students to select one superpower that they would like to expand on or become even better at, so my example was to improve my public speaking by giving a TED talk.

I'd set a clear and powerful intention but I wasn't sure I was ready to do anything about it back then and it would be four years before I even considered actually putting in an application.

But the intention had been set and was there all the same and that's the moment when the wheels had been put into motion. Little by little I began finding opportunities to speak at other events and then I started putting myself forward for speaking opportunities. The next thing I knew I was being invited to speak internationally; first Paris, then London, then the Australian Embassy to Portugal.

Then life started putting the right people in front of me. Everything from women who had given TED talks to women who were TEDtalk speaking coaches to women who shared the same dream as me of speaking at TEDx, it was incredible how the coincidences kept coming up. It was as if by setting the intention I was being supported in countless ways to realise it as if by magic.

Looking back I can see all of the steps being laid out like stepping stones across a creek, clear and direct, but success never feels like that when you're living it. In real life, the stones are jagged and slippery and sometimes you fall into the water and get drenched head to toe and have to awkwardly climb back out and scramble back onto the stepping stone before or sometimes go back to the start and try a completely different set of stones!

And this, my friends, is the difference between intentions and goals.

Goal setting is all about writing a plan and having a clear strategy for every step of the way. This is incredibly useful in some situations and as an entrepreneur, something I use all the time.

Intention setting however is a different concept altogether. It's about letting go of the need to control the outcome. It's about being open to receive and letting opportunities flow to you instead of forcing them to happen. It's about action and putting the work in for sure but it's also about trusting the process and allowing the magic to happen in the way that it does, which is not necessarily the same as the picture you originally had in your head. And it's about setting the intention and knowing that everything will unfold exactly as it's meant to. And it's about letting go of the fear, anxiety and self-doubt that stands in the way of us realising our biggest dreams.

You could think of goal setting as a road through a busy city with lots of traffic jams, traffic lights and stop signs in the way of you reaching your pre-determined final destination. Whereas intention setting is more like walking through a leafy green forest path to a clearing and discovering a beautiful, secret picnic spot that you've never been to before.

But back to my TED Talk. I'd set the intention, but that didn't mean that my fears and self-doubt which activate my need for perfection and my inner critic's voice of stay small to stay safe, stay silent and then no one will know that you're an impostor, automatically went away. Learning to let go of trying to control the outcome has been a big lesson for me in understanding how to achieve big dreams and realise my intentions.

So there I was puffy eyed in the bathroom, feeling utterly alone and not knowing how to get out of this space of hopelessness but knowing that I needed to when, 'Ping!' "Oh a message! Who could be messaging me so early in the morning?" A message arrived in a group chat from one of my most intuitive friends who always seems to know when I need her. Her message simply said, "What's in your heart today?" and the way it was worded made me feel as if I could hear her voice in my mind. It prompted me to instantly reply with honesty and vulnerability, not exactly asking for help, but definitely admitting that I was struggling. "I have my second TED meeting today and I'm so lost with what I'm saying." I instantly felt less alone just by saying those words. And then as the group each reached out with reassurance and offers to call me and talk me through it I knew that I would be OK.

It's up to us to set the intention and to work towards realising that dream but we also have to be open to allowing help along the way and receiving support when we need it. There's no shame in this, it's how we were meant to achieve our dreams. We need each other and other people often have the key that unlocks the magic inside of us.

So I called my friend Kathy, who happened to be a TED coach, and we had a strategy talk about the structure of the talk, the main message I wanted to convey and how to bring in the elements of storytelling combined with the research to create a powerful and compelling presentation.

I went into that second meeting with confidence in myself and my message and when it was over I came out of there triumphant and smiling.

"An intention is the starting point of every dream and idea that you plan or intend to carry out. If you mean something, it's an intention. It is a statement that inspires action through mental focus, clarity and a synergy of will." Sara Capacci

I was back on track with my intention with more power than ever behind my focus, clarity and will to achieve it. I had the fire now, to take action and to create the powerful and beautiful message of connection that I wanted to share with the world.

Here's a post I wrote about how I was feeling on social media:

"This Saturday is a day I've been dreaming about for many years. I'm finally going to be appearing on stage as a TEDx speaker!

I'm excited, over the moon, nervous and all of the emotions in between! The journey to get here has not been easy and effortless. I've spent hours on writing my speech and learning it but the hardest part has been overcoming my own fears and self-doubt. Overthinking. Believing I wasn't qualified enough, confident enough, knowledgeable enough, clever enough and on and on has made this process so much harder than it needed to be. The key has been to reach out and to ask for help. Yes I've also had to put in the hours for writing and rehearsing but without having the courage to admit I needed help and reach out to people who I knew could help me this all would have been so much harder.

I think the message that people need to hear is that you can do hard things and you can achieve your goals even when they seem impossible, but the first step is acknowledging that it's OK to be afraid and then the second step is knowing that it's OK to ask for help. You never have to do it alone. (My whole TED Talk is about not being alone and yet even I struggled with asking for help!)

The countdown to my big day is now officially on and although I still feel some fear and self-doubt that it will all go as planned or be perfect, I know that I can do this!"

It felt in many ways like I was on a hero's journey and at every point along the way I had to battle with my inner demons, my self-doubt, illusions, false beliefs and insecurities, but I knew that if I stayed committed to my intention I would rise triumphantly at the end.

Setting an intention is an important part of my ability to dream and my ability to dream is an important part of what has made me successful as an entrepreneur.

Dreams can be ethereal and hard to pin down but I've discovered from observing the dreams that others have and from my own experience that there is a logical sequence that dreaming takes. One of the most important things about dreaming is to not let your fears and self-doubt take the wheel, you must be the driver, you must allow your intention to guide you. Quietening fear is often the hardest part of realising your dream as fears will often arise at every step of the journey.

The first step is just to dream. I call this the Daydream phase. In this phase your dream is just an idea. It's something that you've perhaps casually thought of, and you haven't shared with anyone yet. At this stage it's private, it's just for you, you're thinking about it or you're daydreaming about it in quiet moments. Giving a TED Talk was just a daydream before I ever spoke it aloud, it was an idea that maybe that would be something I would like to do. It was a vision of a big red circle on the floor, lots of bright lights, an audience filled with people and me standing on a big stage and sharing my message with the world. It might be as if you're trying it on to see whether that dream is going to work for you, what it feels like, what it looks like and just kind of getting clarity about it, but it's not something that you've even spoken about yet.

The first step to realising your dream is that simple. It's just having that idea and not squashing it or stifling it with negative thoughts and instead allowing it space and time for getting clearer, to grow and to develop. It's important to allow yourself time to enjoy this daydreaming phase. It seems simple but it's a crucial part of the process and essential that you ensure your negative thoughts don't extinguish the flame before it has even begun.

The next phase is the calling in phase, that's where you take your dream, or idea and you speak about it, you begin to give it a little life. You don't have to rush into anything. I want you to just spend some time in this phase, calling it in. This is where you find a friend, and you have a conversation about your dream. Keep it light and test the idea out. Tell them, this is what I would love to do, or if your dream involves someone else, this is where you begin to make plans with them, and you start to give your dream a voice.

A word of caution here, not everyone is the right person to share a dream with first. There are some people who will squash your dream immediately and tell you you're crazy; these are not the right people to share a new dream with. You might have to tell them eventually if they're a close family member or part of your plan but if you think they might be a dream crusher choose someone else to begin with.

I remember calling in my dream by sharing it first with a class of students as part of my presentation. I had a slide in my PowerPoint that went with it and I made speaking my intention to the world a part of the class. Every time I gave that class I would call it in a little more.

In this phase there are some simple rituals that you can try. Creating a vision board is another way to call in your dream, this can be made using cut out pictures from magazines, or printed photos and glued onto a big piece of paper or as a Pinterest board which you add to over time. I prefer making vision boards on paper as I can then frame them and put them in a place in my house where I can see them every day as a visual reminder. I find music helps too and I love to create a playlist with songs related to my dream.

This is your time to visualise, get clear and start speaking about your dream. Get clarity around what it's going to look like, what it's going to feel like and how it's going to go. I encourage you to do something about your dream, put it into words, write about it, tell a friend, create a playlist. Make a Pinterest board, get a vision board going.

There's lots of ways that you can go from just thinking about your dream to start calling it in.

The next step is the action phase and this is where things get serious. The action phase is where you actually do something; you take that first action step towards realising your dream. I call it the five seconds of courage phase because you've actually got to do something. It's all well and good to have a dream and make your vision board and daydream about it, but if you want to make it a reality you've actually got to do something. And that first step is sometimes the hardest. So a great example of that would be when I applied to do my TEDTalk, it was a scary step, I was putting myself out there and the possibility of rejection was very real. There are typically hundreds of applications for TEDx events and only limited spaces. For the event I spoke at there were only eight. This took courage and I almost didn't do it because it's typically a written application as well as a video submission of a two-minute summary of your topic. I spent hours on researching and preparing my written and video application and I was so proud of myself for submitting it.

So whatever that first action step looks like for you, that's where you begin; it will be different for everyone depending on what your dream is but that's the first step, just to take that action, that five seconds of courage. If there's something that you're thinking about doing, what's going to be that first step, what's going to take that five seconds of courage that you're going to need to just do that thing and make things happen and make a start.

The next step is the focus phase. And this is where the hard work comes in. It's lovely to have a dream but unless you're going to take action, unless you're going to make things happen, it will just stay a dream. You do have to do the work.

So, whatever your dream is, it's going to take focus and hard work and you're going to have setbacks and challenges, but you're also going to have success. This was definitely my experience with my TEDTalk preparation, I put in hours of work. Every morning I would be up early first writing my speech and then once I'd got to my final draft (Draft 7!) I began rehearsing, practising and memorising my words. I trained every day for three weeks in the lead up to the event, performing in front of the mirror, for my dog, my children, clients and friends, everyone became my audience as I got ready to take the stage. A lot of fear and self-doubt came through in this phase, more than I was expecting because this dream was a such a big thing for me but I allowed myself to feel the feelings and reassure myself that I was on the right path and I was worthy enough to take this chance and I pushed through it. If you can stay focused on your intention, and you're persistent and determined and prepared to put in whatever it takes to get that work done you will reach your goal. This is where you take the steps and do the work. It's simple, but it's not easy and you will be tested and that's OK.

The final step is the reward phase, this is the part where your dreams come true. How amazing is that feeling of when something you've been dreaming about becomes a reality? There's nothing better! Sometimes setting an intention and seeing it materialise can take years but sometimes it will happen fast. No matter what, a big part of the process is to feel good, stay positive and enjoy the journey all the way through because there's so much to learn along the way and often the journey is just as important as the destination.

If you follow all the steps, put in the work, stay focused on your intention, you're persistent, you're resilient, you overcome your challenges, fears and doubts and you use your creativity, then eventually you will get there.

I'll always remember that moment when I walked out onto that stage and took my place in the centre of the red circle of light. I paused and looked out at the audience in wonder and took a moment to just soak in the incredible energy, power and magic of this one perfect moment that had finally arrived. And then I began and I felt the audience travel with me on my journey, it was so silent you could hear a pin drop as they listened, captivated to every word and then the roar of applause as I came to my end. I stood there a moment longer at the end too, basking in the pride I had for myself for having the courage to see this through. I'd nailed it! The feeling of euphoria of stepping off that stage and knowing that I had claimed victory on this, at times, seemingly impossible task was like no other!

Setting an intention takes courage, but I believe if you can dream it you can do it! Yes it will be hard, yes there will be times you are afraid, yes there will be challenges and setbacks, I'm not going to sugar coat it for you, but there will also be magic! Often the learning, personal development and growth that you will experience along the way will be just as important a reward as achieving your goal. So set your intentions boldly, do not be afraid to go after whatever it is your heart is calling you to do, this is your time! Go forth and make your dreams happen!

Add to the conversation.
Share your thoughts on intention below:

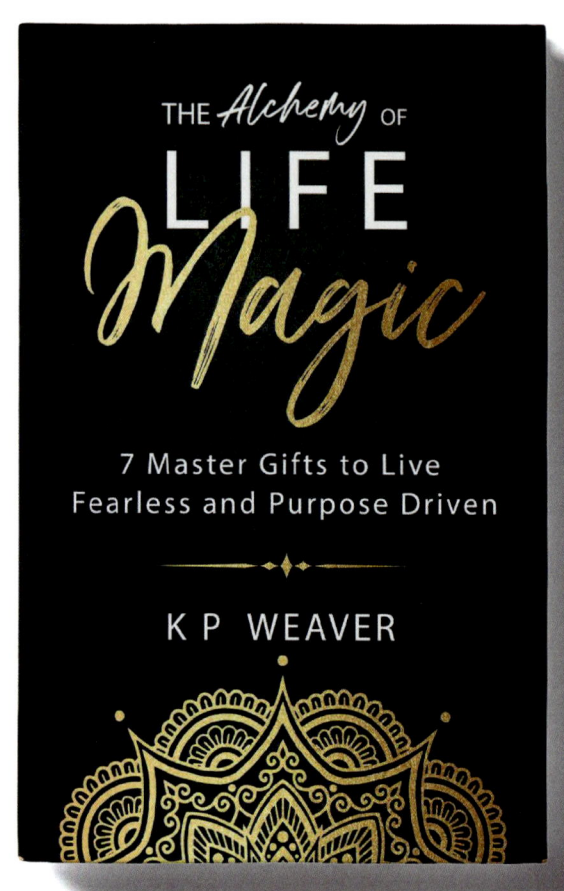

Coming 2022

The Alchemy of Life Magic Series:

The Magic of Mindfulness

The Power of Knowing

The Miracle of Intent

The Gift in Gratitude

The Law of Love

The Freedom in Forgiveness

The Beauty in Belief

www.ingramcontent.com/pod-product-compliance
Lightning Source LLC
Chambersburg PA
CBRC090934010526
44108CB00056B/138